OM NAMAH SHIVAYA

A Powerful Mantra for Mastering Five Elements

AF601819

Prof. (Dr.) Jai Paul Dudeja

INDIA · SINGAPORE · MALAYSIA

Notion Press Media Pvt Ltd

No. 50, Chettiyar Agaram Main Road,
Vanagaram, Chennai, Tamil Nadu – 600 095

First Published by Notion Press 2022
Copyright © Prof. (Dr.) Jai Paul Dudeja 2022
All Rights Reserved.

ISBN 979-8-88546-869-5

This book has been published with all efforts taken to make the material error-free after the consent of the author. However, the author and the publisher do not assume and hereby disclaim any liability to any party for any loss, damage, or disruption caused by errors or omissions, whether such errors or omissions result from negligence, accident, or any other cause.

While every effort has been made to avoid any mistake or omission, this publication is being sold on the condition and understanding that neither the author nor the publishers or printers would be liable in any manner to any person by reason of any mistake or omission in this publication or for any action taken or omitted to be taken or advice rendered or accepted on the basis of this work. For any defect in printing or binding the publishers will be liable only to replace the defective copy by another copy of this work then available.

This book is a humble dedication to
Late Swami Muktananda ji of Siddha Peeth, Ganeshpuri,
where I was initiated to this Magic Mantra

Contents

Preface

Dear Readers,

I am extremely happy to see this book titled, **"Om Namah Shivaya: A Powerful Mantra for Mastering Five Elements"** in your hands. It is my firm belief that you have chosen to read this book with a specific aim in mind, and I assure you that you will not be disappointed.

Om Namah Shivaya is one of the most powerful mantras. The chanter of this mantra gets miraculous benefits at the physical, mental and spiritual levels. Namah Shivaya means "Salutation to Lord Shiva". It is called Panchakshara mantra, meaning that it is the "five-syllable" mantra (excluding the Om) Na, Ma, Shi, Va, Ya. Here 'Na' represents earth; 'Ma' represents water; 'Shi' represents fire; 'Va' represents Pranic air; and 'Ya' represents sky or ether. For this reason, this mantra is known for mastering all these five elements in the Universe. It is not just a moksha giving mantra; it also enlightens, our inner thought-process and improves blood circulation and has a positive effect on the neurons. It increases the happiness molecule which is known as GABA chemical. The list of incredible benefits of chanting Om Namah Shivaya mantra is very large. For example, it gives the chanter freedom from stress, depression and lethargy. It is claimed that the chanter of 'Om Namah Shivaya' need not do any other spiritual practices to attain peace, happiness, bliss and enlightenment.

The book consists of **seven chapters.**

The **first chapter** titled, "Introduction to 'Om Namah Shivaya' Mantra", introduces and overviews this powerful mantra. It is a must-read for all. The **second chapter** titled, "Maha Shiva Purana or Shiva Purana" describes this mantra mentioned in this Purana. The **third chapter** titled, "'Om Namah Shivaya': Meaning and Significance" describes in detail the significance and various other aspects of this mantra. The **fourth chapter** titled, "About Lord Shiva" mentions, in details, the physical and conceptual aspects of Shiva. The **fifth chapter** titled, "Research on 'Om Namah Shivaya' Mantra" mentions some of the research work done on this mantra. The **sixth chapter** titled "Om Namah Shivaya-Based Meditation (Japa)" describes the procedure of meditation/Japa of 'Om Namah Shivaya' mantra. And finally the last and the **seventh chapter** titled, "Beneficial Effects of 'Om Namah Shivaya' Mantra" is a genuine marketing effort to sell this idea to a large number of seekers who can benefit from this great mantra.

The author sincerely believes that a book of this nature will be useful for all the readers across the globe who wish understand the significance of this powerful mantra, and get physical, mental and spiritual benefits by chanting it.

I would gratefully and open heartedly love to receive any encouraging/critical comments as well as feedback from my dear readers at my Email ID: drjpdudeja@gmail.com

Sincerely

2022 **Prof. (Dr.) Jai Paul Dudeja**

Acknowledgements

The seeds of my interest in 'various mantras' were sown more than sixty years ago by my revered parents, **Late (Dr.) Shanti Sawrup Dudeja and Late (Mrs.) Jai Devi Dudeja**. I bow to them, wherever they are in the other world.

I have greatly benefitted in going through the books and articles referred in the 'Bibliography' in this Book. I gratefully acknowledge these authors for enhancing my understanding on the subject matter of this book.

Last but not the least, my greatest admiration is reserved for **Mrs. Rita Dudeja, my wife**, my best friend and my constant source of inspiration, for all my ventures and endeavours like this and many others.

2022 **Prof. (Dr.) Jai Paul Dudeja**

CHAPTER 1

Introduction to 'Om Namah Shivaya' Mantra

1.1 What is Mantra?

The word 'Mantra' comes from the ancient Sanskrit language. 'Man' (pronounced as 'Mun' as in Nun) means mind, and 'tra' means release.

Another interpretation of Mantra is:

"Mananaat traayate iti mantra"

Meaning: That which protects (traayate) the chanter by its constant repetition (chanting), is a Mantra.

Dictionary.com defines a mantra as "a word or formula, as from the veda, chanted or sung as an incantation or prayer".

A mantra is just like the oar of the boat; it is the instrument one uses to cross the samsära (world) of one's restless mind, with its unending thought waves. The mantra can also be compared to a ladder that you climb to reach the heights of God realization.

Any thought, idea or technique, which removes blindness of mind, is known as mantra. A mantra is a sound, a word, or a phrase, that is recited repetitively, usually in an unvarying tone, and is used as an object of concentration or contemplation for calming the mind. The mantra may be chanted aloud, or recited silently or even thought about silently. Words/syllables of Mantras can be meaningful or meaningless (just a sound) and they may or may not be associated with particular spiritual or religious systems. A mantra is a combination of transcendental sounds meant to release the mind from all the anxieties of material life. One gets miraculous benefits by making use of the causal energy of Mantra.

The importance of Mantra is beautifully explained in '*Yoga* Vashishtha', as follows:

> *Bhavanavashata karyakrama main paralvadayya.*
>
> – Yoga Vashishtha (6/1/81/39)

Meaning: Just as by eating yellow myrobalan (a fruit of yellow colour) the digestion system sets in more quickly and thus diarrhoea ensues; in the same way Mantra chanting with steadfastness and powerful sentiments influences the body at a momentous pace. So, mantra can be said to cure the mental constipation and unblock all the knots from it.

1.2 Mantra Yoga

Mantra occupies a prominent place in Vedic religion and Indian Culture. Since time immemorial saints, seers, sages and Yogis have been practicing Mantra Yoga for spiritual enlightenment. Vedas, the core of Indian culture consist of various mantras for the accomplishment of various purposes. Mantras are used as sacred sounds or utterances. Since they are taken from the sacred texts, they are considered auspicious and God in word form. They are used in ritual and spiritual practices and various sacrificial ceremonies. We have the description of 16 types of samskaras or ceremonies in Vedic scriptures. Each ceremony is performed with a different mantra. Our every festival is celebrated by chanting different mantras. We can't imagine of the celebration of any festivals and ceremonies without the chanting of mantras in Vedic religion.

Mantras are used both for the attainment of physical, material and spiritual goals and purposes. There are various types of mantras like Om Namo Bhagavate Vasudevaya, ***Om Namah Shivaya***, the Mahamrityunjaya mantra, the Gayatri mantra etc. These are common mantras or universal mantras, which anybody can use for a specific purpose. The Maha Mrityunjaya Mantra (for increasing health of body and mind) and the Gayatri Mantra (for increasing creative energy and pranic energy) are examples of this. Anyone may choose to adopt and chant these mantras.

OM is considered the source (basis) of all the mantras. It is the highest and the purest and Brahman himself in word form (Shabda Brahma). It is also known as mantra Purusha (God as mantra). It has the potency to divinize and purify all other verbal expressions and word forms. Hence, it is often used as a prefix to all other mantras to infuse them divine power and purity. Therefore, Mantras constitute the core of Vedic religion and the divine culture of India. The significance of 'OM' will be discussed in details later in this book.

1.2.1 Meaning, Concept and Importance of a Mantra

A mantra is a revealed word, a divine sound that has been received or experienced by Vedic seers in the state of deep meditation and trance. It is a condensed form of spiritual divine energy. Mantra is a sacred formula, it is a subtle form of a deity, sound/vibration. Mantra refers to a "mystical formula" regarding some deity. That is called Mantra by the meditation (Manana) on which the Jiva or the individual soul attains freedom from sin, enjoyment in heaven and final liberation, and by the aid of which it attains in full the fourfold fruit (Purushartha chatustya), i.e., Dharma, Artha, Kama and Moksha.

a. Lord Krishna says: Among words I am the sacred syllable OM. Among offerings, I am the offering of Japa (chanting of mantra or sacred formulas.

b. Maharshi Patanjali says: OM is the word denoting God. Pranav (OM) is the crown of all mantras. We should contemplate it again and again as it is a great power [4].

c. Swami Vivekananda very brilliantly argues: What are Mantras? The whole of this universe has, according to Indian philosophy, both name and form (Nāma-Rupa) as its conditions of manifestation. In the human microcosm, there cannot be a single wave in the mind-stuff (Chitta vritti) unconditioned by name and form. If it be true that nature is built throughout on the same plan, this kind of conditioning by name and form must also be the plan of the building of the whole of the cosmos. "As one lump of clay being known, all things of clay are known", so the knowledge of the microcosm must lead to the knowledge of the macrocosm.

Form of the mantra is the outer crust, of which the name or the idea is the inner essence or kernel. The body is the form, and the mind or the Antahkarana is the name, and sound-symbols are universally associated with Nāma (name) in all beings having the power of speech. In the individual man the thought-waves rising in the limited Mahat or Chitta (mind-stuff), must manifest themselves, first as words, and then as the more concrete forms. In the universe, Brahmā or Hiranyagarbha or the cosmic Mahat first manifested himself as name, and then as form, i.e. as this universe. All this expressed the form, behind which stands the eternal inexpressible Sphota, the manifester as Logos or Word. This eternal Sphota, the essential eternal material of all ideas or names is the power through which the Lord creates the universe, nay, the Lord first becomes conditioned as the Sphota, and then evolves Himself out as the yet more concrete sensible universe. This Sphota has one word as its only possible symbol, and this is the 'Om', it is out of this holiest of all holy words, the mother of all names and forms, the eternal Om, that the whole universe may be supposed to have been created.

a. Sri Raman Maharshi observes: Mantras (repeating sacred syllables) or formula as a means to realize the Self. The mind is a channel, a swift current of thoughts. A mantra is a bund or dam put up in the way of this current to divert the water where it is needed.

b. Sri Aurobindo remarks: The theory of the Mantra is that it is a word of power born out of the secret depths of our being where it has been brooded upon by a deeper consciousness than the mental, framed in the heart and not constructed by the intellect, held in the mind, again concentrated on by the waking mental consciousness and then thrown out silently or vocally — the silent word is perhaps held to be more potent than the spoken — precisely for the work of creation.

c. The Mantra can not only create new subjective states in ourselves, alter our psychical being, reveal knowledge and faculties we did not possess before, can not only produce similar results in other minds than that of the user, but can produce vibrations in the mental and vital atmosphere which result in effects, in actions and even in the production of material forms on the physical plane. Mantra is creation by Word. The word is a sound expressive of the idea. In the supra-physical plane when an idea has to be realized, one can by repeating the word-expression of it, produce vibrations which prepare the mind for the realization of the idea. That is the principle of the Mantra and of japa. One repeats the name of the Divine and the vibrations created in the consciousness prepare the realization of the Divine. It is the same idea that is expressed in the Bible, "God said, let there be Light, and there was Light." It is creation by the Word.

d. Swami Vishnu-Devananda says: "A mantra is a mystical energy encased in a sound structure... It steadies the mind and leads to the stillness of meditation."

e. As stated by swami Satyananda Saraswati: Mantras are "purpose-specific", that is, each mantra, whether Bija or a more elaborate construction of separate mantra, is used to realize specific results. Health, prosperity, spiritual realization and social stability are examples of such objectives. As a result, individuals choose to recite or chant different mantras according to their needs. It is important to note however, that one must never alter the mantra. If done, it is no longer a mantra and its power is lost. It becomes just sounds. Also, Mantra Japa must be done mindfully and with respect. The practice should be regular and exist for the practitioner with the same observances as is given to other daily practices. For example, we typically follow a specific schedule concerning our diet. This is done to ensure proper and constant nutrition to our bodies. We should treat mantras the same way. It should be done regularly at prescribed times and for a specific length of time. In this way, we can expect to gain realization through the mantras transformative inner power. As the Rishis sat in meditation and reached higher levels, they received the sounds known as mantra. Mantras, therefore, are not a creation of the human mind. They were perceived from higher sources. In Islam it is said that the Koran was revealed by God, which means that whoever received the Koran had attained a very high yogic state. In the same way, Christians speak of the Bible as a revealed scripture. Sanatana Dharma, the eternal Vedic religion, too is understood as having been revealed. The Vedas were not written by any man. This, however, does not mean that the pen that wrote them was held in God's hand; it only means that they were revealed to Rishis in the transcendental state. The same is said about the Ramacharitamanas.

1.2.2 Elements of Mantra

There are five elements of a Mantra. They are: Rishi (Seer), Chhanda (meter), Devata (deity), Bija (seed), and Tattva (element).

a. Rishi (Seer): There were ancient seers and sages, who had the actual realization of mantra. In meditation, when the rishis were able to transcend the material consciousness, rising to a very high level, those sounds heard by them in that highest state were called mantra. Every Mantra has a Rishi. Rishi means the seer who got that mantra through divine vision (darshana) for the first time and got siddhi or perfection in that mantra. Some rishis also discover mantras, and then they become the rishi of that mantra. The seer is a spiritual scientist who firstly makes experiments with mantra in the laboratory of his own body, mind and spirit and there after he helps others in making such experiments.

b. Chanda: Meter, which is technically very specific for each mantra. It is actual pronunciation of that mantra and its meter or the science behind the meter. That is "how" the pronunciation of the sound (mantra) while doing japa. It is how to say the mantra in a particular rhythm so the deity is pleased. It is the rhythm to be followed to chant a mantra. All mantras are named traditionally with a Chhandas.

c. Devata: The deity of the mantra or governing deity of a mantra. Every mantra has a devata. The devata is invoked by the mantra to come into the heart. There are so many streams of supreme consciousness in this vast universe. The aspirant attracts the stream of consciousness of that particular deity of that mantra as rays of the light.

d. Bija: The seed syllable that created the mantra and contains the mantra within itself, like the seed that creates the tree. Every mantra has a bija (seed syllable) from which it sprouts or originates, which creates the mantra. Bija mantras are used to awaken the different energy centres located in the human body. ***Namah Shivaya*** comes from the bija 'Haum'. Hare Krishna maha mantra comes from "Kleem'. Hrim, shrim, klim, Aiam, Hoom, Yum, Bum, Rum, Lum etc are some of the bija mantras which can be called subtle injections used to inject some additional power in a mantra. As per the need, such bija mantras are added to mantras. We call them potential mantras, because they contain dormant, potential energy of different forces. Each of the powers or forces in the world has its own bija mantra. Those bija mantras are just like little bombs, the type of time bomb which explodes just at the right moment. Just as you plant a seed in the earth and from that a giant tree grows up, giving thousands of fruits, such is the power of the bija mantra. With the practice of Anushthana, prolonged mantra repetition for a fixed period of time and number of malas, and regular sadhana, the power of the mantra is awakened. When that power is awakened, the consciousness takes the form of the mantra and then the real work of the mantra begins.

e. Tattva: Element is a character of a mantra. It can also be called the key to the mantra. It is the destination to be reached by firm resolution of the aspirant. Every mantra possesses the nature of a particular element (such as Earth, Water, Fire, Air and the sky) and a particular guna (such as Sat, raj and tam). Even elements are worshiped as per the nature of the mantra. Thus each mantra has a seer (rishi) who composed it, a rhythm or meter (Chhanda) which determines its sound, and a deity (devata) who presides over it and manifests when the mantra is correctly pronounced. It also contains a seed syllable (bija) which imparts to it manifesting power (Shakti) and a support (tattva) which makes it strong or stable until it delivers the intended result.

1.2.3 Limbs of Mantra Yoga

There are 16 limbs of Mantra yoga which ensure the aspirant' success on the path of mantra yoga. They are as follows:

Bhakti (devotion)- Faith and devotion to the mantra and the deity is the most important condition to succeed in mantra yoga. Shuddhi (purification) refers to self-purification. It stands for the purification of the body, mind and spirit. It also stands for the purification of the place and direction.

Asana: Refers to that thing on which the aspirant sits. Asanas made of woollen, kusha, resham, Mriga-charma, baghambar, blanket etc. are considered good. Asana also stands for some particular, steady, comfortable postures in which the aspirant sits while chanting Mantra.

Panchang Sevan: Gita, Sahasranam, Stavan, Kavach and Hridaya nyasa are collectively known as Panchang sevan. Gita—that which is sung. Sahasranam means experiencing the vastness of the Supreme Being. Stuti is experiencing the vastness and associating it with the heart. Kavach is having protection from the obstacles arising from sadhana. Hridaya nyasa- is entering the mysteries of Mantra through the heart.

Achara (conduct): Aspirant should bear a good moral conduct.

Dharana (concentration): Concentration is binding the mind to one place.

Divyadesh Sevan (self-identification)

Prana Kriya (Pranayama or breath regulation): Prana means breath, ayam is lengthening or widening through control.

When breathing is controlled so as to retain the breath, it is pranayama.

Mudra (hand locks): Mudra can be described as psychic, emotional, devotional and aesthetic gestures or attitudes.

Tarpana (libations): Offering different objects/materials to the deity.

Havan: Is offering oblations to the burning fire of Yagya. Mantra chanting bears no fruit without Havan.

Bali: Sacrificing evils like pride, lust, anger and any other evil habits and practices is Bali.

Yaag: (contemplation and inner worship) Worshiping the deity is called Yaag.

Japa: (chanting) refers to mantra chanting. Japa means the repetition of a mantra so it encompasses all uses of mantras. However, Japa is most commonly associated with a fixed number of repetitions of a mantra. Usually a string of beads, known as a Mala, with a set number of beads would be used to keep count— one repetition per bead. Traditionally, most Malas have 108 "counter" beads. and a "guru" bead used to indicate where to begin and end. Sometimes shorter malas with 54 or 27 beads can be used with longer mantras. The mala used during mantra practice acts as an anchor for the mind. If a bird is flying over the ocean in search of land, it may use a piece of driftwood to rest upon until it finds land. The mala serves the same purpose for the mind as the piece of wood for the bird. It is an anchor. Just as whispered, vocalized and mental repetitions are used to stay with the practice, the mala too is used to stay focused. The movement of the mala keeps track of time and the numbers of repetition.

The movement also holds your mind and does not allow it to slip. So, a mala should always be used during mantra sadhana. There are five different kinds of malas accepted in the yogic tradition – tulsi, rudraksha, Rakta-chandan (red sandalwood), Shweta chandan (white sandalwood), and crystal. Traditionally, it is believed that Vaishnavas use tulsi, Shaivas use rudraksha and Shaktas use crystal. But this is a religious belief; a spiritual aspirant can use any kind of mala to attain different states. Japa is of three kinds. Japa done aloud is the lowest; Japa done in low tones is the middle; Japa done mentally is the best. (Kularnava Tantra 15.54).

a. **Dhyana (meditation):** when concentration becomes deeper it is called meditation. Uninterrupted stream of the content of consciousness is meditation [26-33].

b. **Samadhi (absorption):** Is the state of self-realization. It is the complete absorption of the individual self with the supreme self. In this state the awareness of the external world is absent. There is the experience of the eternal self, akhanda swaroop. This is the level of consciousness called samadhi, trance or turiya. That state becomes Samadhi when there is only the object appearing without the consciousness of one's own self. It may sound a lot but for the sincere practitioner, who continues to practice step-by-step, it all comes together naturally.

1.3 What is the Literal Meaning of 'Om Namah Shivaya' Mantra?

It means, "I salute or bow to Lord Shiva".

1.4 Why is This Mantra Called 'Shiva Panchakshara' Mantra?

Om Namah Shivaya is one of the most popular Hindu mantras and the most important mantra in Shaivism. Namah Shivaya means "O salutations to the auspicious one!", or "adoration to Lord Shiva". It is called Siva Panchakshara, or Shiva Panchakshara or simply Panchakshara meaning the "five-syllable" mantra (excluding the Om) and is dedicated to Lord Shiva. This Mantra appears as 'Na' 'Ma' 'Shi' 'Vā' and 'Ya' in the Shri Rudram hymn which is a part of the Krishna Yajurveda and also in the Rudrashtadhyayi which is a part of the Shukla Yajurveda. So, it is called 'Panchakshara Mantra' because it contains five letters: 'Na' 'Ma' 'Shi' 'Vā' and 'Ya'.

1.5 Origin of the 'Om Namah Shivaya' Mantra

This mantra is present in the **Shri Rudram** hymn which is part of the Krishna Yajurveda. Shri Rudram hymn is taken from two chapters in the fourth book of Taittiriya Samhita of Krishna Yajurveda. Each chapter consists of eleven anuvaka or hymns. Name of both chapters are **Namakam** (chapter five) and **Chamakam** (chapter seven) respectively. The Namakam in Shri Rudram describes the names or epithets of Rudra, who is a fear-inducing aspect of Shiva. The devotee asks for the benevolent aspect of Shiva to be invoked rather than the terrible aspect of Rudra and requests for the forgiveness of sins. The Chamakam (chapter seven) asks for the fulfillment of wishes.

The mantra appears without the initial Om in the eighth hymn of Namakam (Taittiriya Samhita, 4.5.8.1) as Namaḥ śivāya ca śivatarāya ca. This means "Salutations unto Śiva the, auspicious one, unto Śivatara the one whom none more auspicious can exist".

Namakam: The Namakam in particular enumerates the various epithets and names of Rudra. It recognizes the violent aspects of Rudra and requests him to be benevolent and peaceful, rather than violent and destructive. It also acknowledges the presence of the deity in those from all walks of life, be they carpenters (Taittiriya Samhita, 4.5.1.2) or thieves (Taittiriya Samhita, 4.5.3.2).

Chamakam: The Chamakam enumerates the various things one would want in life and requests Rudra to grant them to the devotee. It acknowledges both material and spiritual desires and requests the deity for both. Some verses invoke other deities such as Agni and Vishnu and request them to join in the devotee's prayers to Rudra.

The anuvākas or hymns of Namakam correspond to the eleven hymns of TS 4.5, with the final hymn extended by an additional eight verses, including the Mahamrityunjaya Mantra. The mantra **'Om Namah Shivaya'** is derived from the Shri Rudram, in which it appears in the verses of Taittiriya Samhita, 4.5.8 though without the syllable Om. The anuvākas or hymns of Chamakam correspond to Taittiriya Samhita, 4.7 and they ask God for fulfillment of wishes.

The earliest homage hymns to Rudra is the Śatarudrīya found in the Yajurveda (TS 4.5.1-11, VS 16.1-66).

This mantra also appears in the Rudrashtadhyayi, a part of the Shukla Yajurveda. In the Rudrashtadhyayi, the mantra appears in the 5th chapter (also known as Namakam) verse 41.

1.6 Translations Among Different Traditions

Namah Shivaya means "Adoration to Lord Shiva"; this is preceded by the devotional syllable "Om".

1.6.1: In **Siddha Shaivism and Shaiva Siddhanta Shaivism** traditions, Namah Shivaya is considered as Pancha Bodha Tattva of Lord Shiva and his universal oneness of five elements:

i. 'Na' sound represents earth;

ii. 'Ma' sound represents water;

iii. 'Shi' sound represents fire;

iv. 'Vā' sound represents Pranic air; and

v. 'Ya' sound represents sky or ether.

Its total meaning is that "universal consciousness is one".

1.6.2 In **Shaiva Siddhanta**, the five letters also represent:

i. 'Na' is the Lord's concealing grace;

ii. 'Ma' is the world;

iii. 'Shi' stands for Shiva;

iv. 'Vā' is His revealing grace; and

v. 'Ya' is the Ātman or soul.

1.6.3 The **Tirumantiram** (a scripture in Shaiva Siddhanta) announces that "His feet are the letter 'Na'. His navel is the letter 'Ma'. His shoulders are the letter 'Shi'. His mouth, the letter 'Vā'. His radiant cranial centre aloft is 'Ya'. Thus is the five-lettered form of Shiva.": Tirumantiram 941.

1.7 Panchakshari Mantra in Different Scriptures

1. The Mantra appears as 'Na' 'Ma' 'Shi' 'Vā' and 'Ya' in the Shri Rudram hymn which is a part of the Krishna Yajurveda. Thus predates the use of Shiva as a proper name, in the original context being an address to Lord Rudra (later Shiva), where Shiva retains its original meaning as an adjective, meaning "auspicious, benign, friendly", a euphemistic epithet of Rudra.

2. The mantra appears in the Rudrashtadhyayi which is a part of the Shukla Yajurveda.

3. Whole Panchakshara Stotra is dedicated to this mantra.

4. Tirumantiram, a scripture written in Tamil language, speaks of the meaning of the mantra.

5. It appears in the Shiva Purana in the chapter 1.2.10 (Shabda-Brahma Tanu) and in its Vidyeshvara samhita and in chapter 13 of the Vayaviya samhita of the Shiva Purana as Om Namaḥ Śivāya. It is also referenced many times throughout the Śiva Purana as the "5 syllable Mantra" and "6 syllable mantra" when including Om.

6. The Tamil Saivaite hymn Tiruvacakam begins with the five letters 'Na' 'Ma' 'Shi' 'Vā' and 'Ya'.

1.8 Sri Rudram

The Sri Rudram occurs in Krishna Yajur Veda in the Taithireeya Samhita in the fourth and seventh chapters. This prayer to Rudra has two parts-the **Namakam** (verses ending with Nama) and the **Chamakam** (Verses ending with Cha May) each with eleven sections. It is also known as Satha Rudreeyam or Rudra Prasnam. While Namakam is a prayer to Rudra to forget about his avenging fierce, fearful and horrendous form and turn himself into a peaceful form and do good to us, Chamakam on the other hand lists out the blessings to be got from a prayer to Rudra and prays Him to regulate and bless our life for a moment forgetting his anger. This also has eleven parts.

1.8.1 Meaning of the Word Rudra

There are Several meanings to the word Rudra:

Rtam (dam) Samsaara dukham draava yat iti Rudrah.

Meaning: He destroys the sorrows of the world, that is, (Rudra).

Rodati Sarvamantakala

Meaning: The one who makes one to suffer.

Rtou Naadaante dravati - draavayateeti Rudrah.

Meaning: The end note of the musical sound, that is, (Rudra).

Rtya - Vedarupaya, dharmadinava-loka yati praayateeti vaa Rudrah.

Meaning: In the form of Veda Dharma is promoted, that is, (Rudra).

Rtya-vaagrupaya, vaakyam, prapayateeti Rudrah.

Meaning: In the form of Speech, brings out the importance of the meaning of words, that is, (Rudra).

Rtya-Pranava rupaya svatmanam prayateeti Rudrah.

Meaning: In the name of pranava (OM) He makes one to realize him.

Rudroroutiti satye rorupamaano dravati pravashati martyaaniti Rudrah.

Meaning: In the form truth he enters humans.

Rtam Sabdam Vedaatmaanam Brahmane dadati Kalpaadaaviti Rudrah.

Meaning: Rudra presented Vedas to Brahma at the Commencement of kalpa. Rudras also means the persons created by Rudra as Sadrusha.

Rtim Raati is responsible for the sound. He is praṇa Svarupa. Granter of praṇa (life).

Meaning: Rudram is for example light, Teja and Ruth who binds and attracts.

Taam bhakte draavayati.

Meaning: He is even capable of driving away hat Shakti (energy).

1.8.2 Birth of Rudra

There are also several stories about the birth of Rudra. Some of them are:

Brahma created first four rishis called Sananda, Sanaka, Sanatana and Sanat Kumara with a view to initiate the activities of creation. But all the four preferred to be ascetics and never bothered to reproduce. Then Brahma got so angry that the anger was sufficient to burn all the three worlds. This anger escaped from his eyebrows and took the form of Rudra. Rudra's form was half woman and half man. Brahma commanded to divide and disappeared. Rudra divided himself into Rudra the male part as well as Rudhrani the female part. This male part further got divided in to eleven parts. They were Ajan, Ekaath, Ahirbudhnyan, Twashta, Rudra, Hara, Sambhu, Tryambaka, Aparajitha, Easana and Tribhuvana. The female aspect was called Rudrani and she also divided herself into eleven parts and became consort to the eleven Rudras.

From Brahma's anger was born the Rudra, from his lap Narada, from his right Thumb Daksha, from his mind the Sanaka and from his left thumb one daughter called Veeraani.

When Brahma was deep in prayer requesting for a son similar to him, a baby deep blue in colour came on to his lap. That son started crying and Brahma told him not to cry- "Maa Ruda "The child wanted a name. Since he was crying (rudha), he was called Rudra. The child cried another seven times asking for names and another seven Rudras were formed.

1.8.3 First Prayer in the Veda Addressed to Rudra

The first prayer in the Vedas addressed to Rudra occurs in the Rig Veda and it is composed by Sage Kanva and reads as follows:

Kadrudraaya prachetasey meelhustamaaya tavyasey.
Vocheyma shantam hridey.

Meaning: We sing this praise from our hearts of the great Rudra, who is a pourer for the sake of peace.

1.8.4 Panchakshari Mantra

This mantra is the foremost among the mantras contained in Rudram and is the most often chanted mantra among Shaivites: **Om Namah Shivaya**

1.8.5 Eleven Anuvaakas

The Sri Rudram is divided into eleven sections called anuvaakas.

In the **first anuvaaka** consisting of eleven sukthaas, Rudra is requested by the devotee to turn his fierce exterior and not use his weapons on his devotees. He is also requested to annihilate the sins committed by his devotees.

In the **second anuvaaka** consisting of two sukthaas the Rudra is part of nature in all its glory as plants and medicinal herbs. He is requested to untie the bonds of the day-to-day life.

The **third anuvaaka** consisting of two sukthaas describe Rudra as a thief. He might have been presumed to be the stealer of ignorance from us.

In the **fourth anuvaaka,** consisting of two sukthaas, Rudra is the common man with his deficiencies, angularities and described as the creator and worker of all kinds.

In the **fifth Anuvaaka,** consisting of two sukthaas, several aspects of Rudra's personality, especially as God responsible for creation, preservation and destruction is described.

In the **sixth anuvaaka** consisting of two sukthaas. Rudra is identified with changes of his personality over eons of time and the roles he has played in different ages. He is described as the source of the different worlds, Shrutis (Vedas) and its essence in Vedanta.

In the **seventh anuvaaka**, consisting of two sukthaas, his all-pervading presence in nature in all its fury and majesty is described.

In the **eighth anuvaaka**, Rudra is described as He who illumines other Gods and confers powers on them. The Panchakshari mantra viz. **"Nama Shivaya" occurs for the first time in Vedas in this anuvaaka.**

In the **ninth anuvaaka,** which consists of two sukthaas, the unfancied and hard to live places where Rudra lives is listed out. In essence it means he is all pervasive.

In the **tenth** anuvaaka, Rudra is again requested not to show his furious fear giving form and appear before the devotee in a peaceful calm form. The mantras unlike the ones till ninth anuvaaka do not end in Nama after every description.

In the **eleventh anuvaaka**, consisting of eleven sukthaas, Rudra's army called Ganaas is praised and they, wherever they exist, are beseeched to protect the devotees of Rudra.

This anuvaaka is followed by six stotras of Rudra.

1.8.6 Methods of Chanting Rudra

The Chamakam, lists out the blessings that can be got by prayer to Rudra. The reading or chanting of Rudra is said to be complete only when **Chamakam** also is chanted. There are five methods of chanting Rudra viz:

i. Ordinary method where first Rudram is read and then Chamakam.

ii. Rudra ekadasini, where after chanting Rudram, the first anuvaaka of Chamakam is chanted, again after chanting Rudram the second anuvaaka of Chamakam is chanted and so on till the eleventh chanting of Rudram followed by eleventh anuvaaka of Chamakam.

iii. Laghu Rudram, where Rudra ekadasini is chanted eleven times.

iv. Maha Rudram, where Laghu Rudram is chanted eleven times.

v. Athi Rudram, where Maha Rudram is chanted eleven times.

1.9 Usage of 'Om Namah Shivaya' Mantra

This mantra is repeated verbally or mentally, drawing the mind in upon itself to Lord Shiva's infinite, all-pervasive presence. Traditionally it is repeated **108 times** a day while keeping count on a strand of rudraksha beads. This practice is called japa yoga. It is freely sung and chanted by everyone, but it is most powerful when given by one's guru. Before this initiation which is called mantra diksha, the guru will usually require a period of study. This initiation is often part of a temple ritual, such as a puja, japa, homa (fire ceremony), dhyana or and while smearing vibhuti. The guru whispers the mantra into the disciple's right ear, along with instructions on how and when to chant it.

1.10 Spiritual and Scientific Significance of the Number 108

1.10.1 Introduction to Number 108

Have you ever wondered why are we advised by our elders, priests, pundits or even the ancient scriptures, to chant a particular mantra (hymn), Om Namah Shivaya', for example, precisely 108 times to reap its targeted benefits? When we react back and point out that counting the number of chants consciously will distract our focus or our attention from our concentration or contemplation etc., and thus dilute the desired benefits of the mantra; we are given an alternative to take the help of a rosary (or maala) which contains 108 beads (besides a Guru bead at the beginning). Vedic sages devised a Vijanati maala (rosary) with 108 beads/stones to keep count of mantras in their daily ritual of meditation. This maala is usually made of the materials like rudraksha (linked to Lord Shiva) or tulsi or whatever. By holding one bead at a time per mantra repetition (japa or chanting) we can concentrate our attention on the mantra and not on its counting. The number 108 is very auspicious for the followers of Sanatana Dharma. Vedic sages used the term 'Shri 108' to represent yogis, preceptors, divine and highly learned gurus. The number of flowers in a vara maala (wedding garland) is also 108 and same is the number in vrata (fasting) maala. Ancient sages from the Vedic traditions recognized that 108 is a 'Harshad Number' in that it is divisible by the sum of its digits. In Sanskrit, Harshad means 'Joy-Giver'.

We describe here the spiritual and scientific significance of this wonderful number '108'.

1.10.2 Number 108 in Hinduism

1.10.2.1 According to yogic tradition, there are 108 pithas, or sacred sites, throughout India.

1.10.2.2 There are 108 Upanishads and 108 Puranas. The Upanishads are a collection of Hindu texts, which contain some of the central philosophical concepts of Hinduism. There are 10 Upanishads associated with Rig Veda, 50 Upanishads associated with Yajurveda, 16 Upanishads associated with Sama veda, and 32 Upanishads associated with Atharva veda; thus making a total of 108 Upanishads. The Puranas are a vast genre of Hindu texts that encyclopedically cover a wide range of topics, particularly myths, legends and other traditional lore. Composed primarily in Sanskrit, but also in regional languages, several of these texts are named after major Hindu deities such as Vishnu, Shiva and Devi etc.

1.10.2.3 There are 54 letters in Sanskrit each can be mentioned as masculine (Shiva) and feminine (Shakti) aspect, thus totaling to 108.

1.10.2.4 Hindus have 108 forms of dance. Lord Shiva was fond of dancing (Nataraj). He danced in 108 mudras (poses) and thus making 108 as the unit of creation.

1.10.2.5 River Ganga: The sacred River Ganga spans a longitude of 12 degrees (79 to 91), and latitude of 9 degrees (22 to 31). 12 times 9 equal 108.

1.10.2.6 Heart Chakra: The chakras are the intersections of energy lines, and there are said to be a total of 108 energy lines converging to form the heart chakra. One of them, sushumna leads to the crown chakra, and is said to be the path to Self-realization.

1.10.2.7 Sri Yantra: On the Sri Yantra there are marmas where three lines intersect, and there are 54 such intersections. Each intersection has masculine and feminine, shiva and shakti qualities. 54 times 2 equal 108. Thus, there are 108 points that define the Sri Yantra as well as the human body.

1.10.2.8 There are 108 names for Lord Vishnu and 108 names for Lord Shiva.

1.10.2.9 In both Hindu and Tibetan traditions, there are 54 energies associated with Shiva and Shakti, male and female energies which manifest as reality. This makes the total (male and female) to 108.

1.10.2.10 There are 108 steps leading to many Hindu temples, signifying that that there are 108 steps to reach God (Paramatma).

1.10.2.11 In Hindu tradition, the Mukhya Shivaganas (attendants of Shiva) are 108 in number and hence Shaiva religions, particularly Lingayats, use maalas of 108 beads for prayer and meditation.

1.10.2.12 Gopis of Krishna: There were said to be 108 gopis or maid servants of Krishna. Recital of their names, often accompanied by the counting of a 108-beaded mala, is often done during religious ceremonies.

1.10.2.13 Pranayama is often completed in cycles of 108.

1.10.2.14 Sun salutations (Surya Namaskar) are often performed in nine rounds of the 12 postures (totaling 108).

1.10.2.15 Parshurama, the sixth avatar of lord Vishnu, installed 108 Dhanvantari idols (god of Ayurveda) after the drying up of river Saraswati.

1.10.3 Significance of Number 108 in Other Areas

1.10.3.1 In Astrology

In Indian astrology we have 12 houses and 9 planets. 12 times 9 equals to 108.

1.10.4 In Astronomy

1.10.4.1 The diameter of the Sun is 108 times the diameter of the Earth.

1.10.4.2 Distance between the sun and is earth is 108 times the diameter of the sun.

1.10.4.3 Distance between the moon and is earth is 108 times the diameter of the moon.

1.10.4.4 Astronomically, there are 27 constellations in our galaxy, and each one them has 4 directions, and 27 * 4 = 108, In other words the number 108 covers the whole galaxy.

1.10.5 In Arithmetic

1.10.5.1 Powers of 1, 2, and 3 in math: 1 to 1st power = 1; 2 to 2nd power = 4 (= 2×2); 3 to 3rd power=27 (= 3x3x3). 1x4x27=108.

1.10.5.2 Perhaps 108 was given special status because of its relationship to the number 9, which also has been considered an important number in Hinduism and other Asian cultures. Some examples follow. When 108 is divided in half the result is 54; 5 + 4 = 9. Half of 54 is 27, and 2 + 7 = 9. When 108 is multiplied by 2, the result is 216; 2+1+6 = 9. When 108 is multiplied by 3 the result is 324; 3+2+4 = 9. And, of course the sum of 1+0+8 is itself 9.

1.11 108 Names of Lord Shiva and Their Corresponding Mantras

1	**Om Shivaya Namah:**	**Always Pure**
2	Om Maheshwaraya Namah:	Lord Of Gods
3	Om Shambhave Namah:	One Who Bestows Prosperity
4	Om Pinakine Namah:	One Who Has A Bow In His Hand
5	Om Shashishekharaya Namah:	God Who Wears The Crescent Moon In His Hair
6	Om Vamadevaya Namah:	God Who Is Pleasing And Auspicious In Every Way
7	Om Virupakshaya Namah:	Lord Shiva With Oblique Eyes
8	Om Kapardine Namah:	The Lord With Thickly Matted Hair
9	Om Nilalohitaya Namah:	The One With Red And Blue Colour
10	Om Shankaraya Namah:	One Who Gives Happiness and Prosperity
11	Om Shulapanaye Namah:	One Who Carries a Trident

Continued...

12	Om Khatvangine Namah:	God Who Carries A Knurled Club (Khatvanga)
13	Om Vishnuvallabhaya Namah:	One Who Is Dear To Lord Vishnu
14	Om Shipivishtaya Namah:	Lord Whose Form Emits Great Rays Of Light
15	Om Ambikanathaya Namah:	Consort of Ambika (Parvati)
16	Om Shrikanthaya Namah:	Lord with Glorious Neck
17	Om Bhaktavatsalaya Namah:	One Who Is Favourably Inclined Towards His Devotees
18	Om Bhavaya Namah:	God Who Is Existence Itself
19	Om Sharvaya Namah:	Remover Of All Troubles
20	Om Trilokeshaya Namah:	Lord Of All The Three Worlds
21	Om Shitikanthaya Namah:	Lord Who Has White Neck
22	Om ShivaPriyaya Namah:	Beloved Of Parvati
23	Om Ugraya Namah:	One Who Has Extremely Fierce Nature
24	Om Kapaline Namah:	One Who Wears A Necklace Of Skulls
25	Om Kamaraye Namah:	Enemy of Kamadeva
26	Om Andhakasurasudanaya Namah:	Lord Who Killed The Asura Andhaka
27	Om Gangadharaya Namah:	God Who Holds The Ganges River In His Hair

28	Om Lalatakshaya Namah:	One Who Has An Eye In The Forehead
29	Om Kalakalaya Namah:	One Who Is The Death Of Death
30	Om Kripanidhaye Namah:	God Who Is The Treasure Of Compassion
31	Om Bhimaya Namah:	One Who Has Fearful Form
32	Om Parashuhastaya Namah:	God Who Holds Axe In Hands
33	Om Mrigapanaye Namah:	God Who Possesses Deer In Hands
34	Om Jatadharaya Namah:	God Who Keeps Tress (Jata)
35	Om Kailashavasine Namah:	Native Of Kailasha Mountain
36	Om Kawachine Namah:	God Who Possess Armour
37	Om Kathoraya Namah:	God Who Has A Strong Body
38	Om Tripurantakaya Namah:	God Who Killed Tripurasura
39	Om Vrishankaya Namah:	God Who Has A Flag With A Symbol Of Bull
40	Om Vrishabharudhaya Namah:	One Who Rides Bull
41	Om Bhasmodhulitavigrahaya Namah:	One Who Applies Ashes All Over The Body
42	Om Samapriyaya Namah:	One Who Loves With Equality

Continued...

43	Om Swaramayaya Namah:	God Who Lives In All Seven Notes
44	Om Trayimurtaye Namah:	One Who Possesses Three Images Form
45	Om Anishwaraya Namah:	One Who Does Not Have Any Lord
46	Om Sarvajnaya Namah:	One Who Knows Everything
47	Om Paramatmane Namah:	Everyone's Own Soul
48	Om Somasuryagnilochanaya Namah:	One Who Has Eyes In The Form Of Sun, Moon and Fire
49	Om Havishe Namah:	He Who Is Wealthy In The Form Of Ahuti
50	Om Yajnamayaya Namah:	Architect Of All Sacrificial Rites
51	Om Somaya Namah:	One Who Includes The Form Of Uma
52	Om Panchavaktraya Namah:	God Of The Five Activities
53	Om Sadashivaya Namah:	One Who Is Eternally Auspicious
54	Om Vishveshwaraya Namah:	Lord Of The Universe
55	Om Virabhadraya Namah:	Who Is Violent, Yet Peaceful
56	Om Gananathaya Namah:	God Of The Ganas
57	Om Prajapataye Namah:	One Who Is The Creator Of Dynasty
58	Om Hiranyaretase Namah:	One Who Emanates Golden Souls

59	Om Durdharshaya Namah:	One who Is Unconquerable
60	Om Girishaya Namah:	Lord Of Mountains
61	Om Kailashaya Namah	God Who lives in Kailash Mountain
62	Om Anaghaya Namah:	He Who Is Pure
63	Om Bujangabhushanaya Namah:	Lord Adorned With Golden Snakes
64	Om Bhargaya Namah:	Lord Who Ends All Sins
65	Om Giridhanvane Namah:	God Whose Weapon Is A Mountain
66	Om Giripriyaya Namah:	Lord Who Is Fond Of Mountains
67	Om krittivasase Namah:	God Who Wears Clothes Of Elephant Skin
68	Om Puraratiaye Namah:	Destroyer of Town Or "Pur" Named Enemy
69	Om Bhagawate Namah:	God Of Prosperity
70	Om Pramathadhipaya Namah:	God Who Is Served By Goblins
71	Om Mrityunjayaya Namah:	Victor Of Death
72	Om Sukshmatanave Namah:	God Who Has A Subtle Body
73	Om Jagadvyapine Namah:	God Who Lives In The World
74	Om Jagadguruve Namah:	Guru Of All The Worlds
75	Om Vyomakeshaya Namah:	Whose Hair Spreads In The Sky
76	Om Mahasenajanakaya Namah:	Father Of Kartikya

Continued...

77	Om Charuvikramaya Namah:	Guardian Of Wandering Pilgrims
78	Om Rudraya Namah:	One Who Gets Sad By The Pain Of Devotees
79	Om Bhutapataye Namah:	Lord Of Panchabhoota or Bhootapreta
80	Om Sthanave Namah:	Firm And Immovable Deity
81	Om Ahirbudhnyaya Namah:	One Who Possesses Kundalini
82	Om Digambaraya Namah:	The God Whose Robes Is The Cosmos
83	Om Ashtamurtaye Namah:	Lord Who Has Eight Forms
84	Om Anekatmane Namah:	God Who Possesses Many Forms
85	Om Satvikaya Namah:	Lord Of Boundless Energy
86	Om Shuddhavigrahaya Namah:	Lord Of Pure Soul
87	Om Shashvataya Namah:	Lord Who Is Eternal And Endless
88	Om Khandaparashave Namah:	Lord Who Wears Broken Axe
89	Om Ajaya Namah:	One Who Is Boundless
90	Om Pashavimochakaya Namah:	Lord Who Releases All Fetters
91	Om Mridaya Namah:	Lord Who Shows Only Mercy
92	Om Pashupataye Namah:	Lord Of Animals
93	Om Devaya Namah:	Lord Of Devas
94	Om Mahadevaya Namah:	Greatest Of The Gods

95	Om Avyayaya Namah:	One Who is Never Subject To Change
96	Om Haraye Namah:	Same As Lord Vishnu
97	Om Bhaganetrabhide Namah:	Lord Who Damaged Bhaga's Eye
98	Om Avyaktaya Namah:	Shiva Who Is Unseen
99	Om Dakshadhwaraharaya Namah:	Destroyer Of Daksha's Conceited Sacrifice (Yagya)
100	Om Haraya Namah:	Lord Who Dissolves All Bondage And Sins
101	Om Pushadantabhide Namah	One Who Punished Pushan
102	Om Avyagraya Namah:	Lord Who Is Steady And Unwavering
103	Om Sahasrakshaya Namah:	One Who Has Limitless Forms
104	Om Sahasrapade Namah:	Lord Who Is Standing And Walking Everywhere
105	Om Apavargapradaya Namah:	Lord Who Gives And Takes All Things
106	Om Anantaya Namah:	One Who Is unending
107	Om Tarakaya Namah:	Lord Who Is Great Liberator Of Mankind
108	Om Parameshwaraya Namah:	The Great God

1.12 Shiva Panchakshara Stotra

Shri Shiva Panchakshara Stotram is a Stotra. Stotras are a type of popular devotional literature and are not bound by the strict rules as some other ancient Indian scriptures, such as the

Vedas. In Sanskrit literature, poetry written for praise of god is called stotras. The Panchakshara literally means "five letters" in Sanskrit and refers to the five holy letters Na, Ma, Śi, Vā and Ya. This is a prayer to Lord Shiva, and is associated with Shiva's Mantra 'Om Namah Shivaya', of which Namah Shivaya is called the Panchakshari Mantra.

Lord Shiva is the main deity in Shaivism school of Hinduism. The holy word chant to worship Him is made of five letters and is popularly called Panchakshara- Na, Ma, Śi, Vā, and Ya. According to Hindu traditions, the human body is considered to be made up of five elements and these holy letters represent these elements. Na Consecrates Prithvi Tattva (Earth element), Ma does the same with Jal Tattva (Water factor) Si energizes Agni Tattva (Fire element) Va energizes Vayu Tattva (Air factor) and finally Ya energizes Akasha Tattva (Sky/Space element).

In this popular Stotra, each of these holy letters is considered as representing Shiva and the Lord is praised for his great qualities.

Indian philosopher Adi Sankaracharya is the author of this stotra.

Stotra And Meanings

Naagendra Haaraaya TriLochanaaya,
Bhasmanggaraagaaya Maheshvaraaya.
Nityaaya Shuddhaaya DigAmbaraaya,
Tasmay ***"Na"*** *kaaraaya Namah Shivaaya...*

Meaning: The great shiva Who has the King of Snakes as His Garland and, has Three Eyes in his face, Whose Body is Smeared with Sacred Ashes and Who is the Great Lord The supreme God. Who is Eternal, Who is ever Pure and Who has the Four Directions as His Clothes, Salutations to that Shiva, Who is represented by syllable "**Na**", the first syllable of the Panchakshara mantra.

Mandaakini Saleela Chandana-Charchitaaya,
Nandiishvara-Pramatha-Naathaya-Maheshvaraaya.
MandaaraPusspa-BahuPusspa-SuPujitaaya,
*Tasmai "**Ma**" kaaraaya Namah Shivaaya...*

Meaning: Who is Worshipped with Water from the River Mandakini and Smeared with Sandal Paste, Who is the Lord of Nandi and of the Ghosts and Goblins, the Great Lord, Who is Worshipped with Mandara and Many Other Flowers, Salutations to that Shiva, Who is represented by syllable "**Ma**", the second syllable of the Panchakshara mantra.

Shivaaya Gauri VadanaAbjaVrnda,
Suryaaya Dakshadvara Naashakaaya.
Shri Neelakanntthaaya Vrissa-Dhvajaaya
*Tasmai "**Shi**" kaaraaya Namah Shivaaya...*

Meaning: Who is Auspicious and Who is like the Sun Causing the Lotus-Face of mother Gauri to Blossom, Who is the Destroyer of the arrogance of Daksha, Who has a Blue Throat and has a Bull as His Emblem, Salutations to that Shiva, Who is represented by syllable "**Shi**", the third syllable of the Panchakshara mantra.

Vasishttha-Kumbhodbhava-GautamaAarya
Munindra-Devaarchita-Shekharaaya,
Chandraarka-Vaishvaanara-Lochanaaya
*Tasmai "**Va**" kaaraaya Namah Shivaaya.*

Meaning: Who is Worshipped by the Best and most Respected Sages like Vasishtha, Agastya and Gautama and also by the Gods and Who is the Crown of the Universe, Who has the Chandra (Moon), Surya (Sun) and Agni (Fire) as His Three Eyes, Salutations to that Shiva, Who is represented by syllable **"Va"**, the fourth syllable of the Panchakshara mantra.

Yakshya Svaruupaaya JataaDharaaya,
Pinaaka Hastaya Sanatanaya.
Divyaaya Devaaya Dig-Ambaraaya,
*Tasmai **"Ya"** kaaraaya Namah Shivaaya...*

Meaning: Salutations to Shiva, who is the spirit of all Yagyas/ Homas (fire offerings and fire worship), Who has matted hair, Who has the pināka bow in His Hand and Who is Eternal, Who is Divine, Who is the Shining One and Who has the Four Directions as His Clothes (signifying that He is ever Free, Salutations to that Shiva, Who is represented by syllable **"Ya"**, the fifth syllable of the Panchakshara mantra.

Panchaaksharamidam Punnyam
Yah Patthet ShivaSamnidhau,
Shivalokam Aavaapnoti
Shivena Saha Muudate...

Meaning: Whoever Recites this Panchakshara hymn in praise of the five syllables of Na-Ma-Shi-Va-Ya; he is near Shiva every time, and Will Attain the Abode of Shiva and enjoy His Bliss.

1.13 The Energetic Field of Om Namah Shivaya

The chant of 'Om Namah Shivaya' is a love song, to ourselves. A love song we sing to our own deepest inner nature. In this song we recognize that we are the source, like a hologram, a piece of god that also represents the whole. In the Siddha yoga lineage (from which this chant comes) it is considered to be the king of all mantras. The intelligent field of conscious energy of which the universe is made, and concentrates into the dense form we know of as matter, is represented by the god Shiva. Shiva is the totality.

Since the ancient Siddhas did not have the language and metaphors of modern physics they represented the unified field of energy of the cosmos through the metaphors they could grasp, metaphors which allowed them to experience this vast field of conscious energy of which we are an interconnected part of. Their metaphor was the god Shiva. Through deep meditation they experienced the universe as Shiva, and themselves as Shiva. Shiva was said to dwell in the heart and be the size of a thumb and be the whole universe! When we chant this mantra we are allowing the sound vibration tune into our true self, which is a manifestation of the universal energy field condensed into the unique and precious mystery of ourselves. The sound vibration of the mantra is said to be a very pure expression of our deepest nature.

The mantra is said to be the five syllable mantra, na ma si va ya. In exploring the manifestations of the absolute the number five comes up. Five toes, fingers, senses, elements, acts etc.. Shiva is said to have five actions, to create, to maintain, to destroy, to conceal, and to gracefully reveal. This mantra purifies our actions and behaviours tuning them to the pure actions of Shiva, of the source. Our five senses of smelling, tasting, seeing, feeling, and hearing are also purified and refined. The different syllables of the chant are said to purify the five elements of our being and the chakras, or centres of subtle energies. The five elements are not literal elements like those of the periodic table, but fundamental ways that we and the world are structured. The solidity of earth, the liquidity of water, the fieriness of fire, the gaseous and invisible nature of air, and lastly ether or the quality of space. The alchemical process of chanting refines and purifies these elements or aspects of our being.

Om is said to be the heart of Lord Shiva. Om resonates in the head in the sixth chakra, located in the′ center of the forehead. It is also referred to as the third eye center. The emotional issues associated with it focus on the right to see. The sixth chakra is also the place of the guru (the one who sheds light on the darkness, another manifestation of our own deep nature) So the first part of the chant keys us into seeing the absolute on very refined levels.

1.14 Benefits of chanting 'Om Namah Shivaya' Mantra

- The Mantra is **Moksha Giver and stabilizes your thoughts** – The Chanting of Om Namah Shivaya is not just moksha giving mantra; It also enlightens, our inner thoughts process and improves blood circulation on the neurons. In medical term, this concept is called neuroplasticity.

- **Mantra makes you feel Light** – Lord Shiva is highly auspicious, When someone chants Om Namah Shivaya, At that moment he becomes AGHORI. Ghor means extreme and, AGhor (Not Ghor) means the one who is not extreme. That's how Shiva makes you feel light inside your heart.

- A significant vibration originates in the subconsciousness part of the mind which gives the feeling of internal ecstasy. Om Namah Shivaya mantra benefits that the Continuous repetition of the divine mantra is the way toward perennial joy.

- Om Namah Shivaya helps in controlling Senses and anxieties Neelakantham is Vairagya founder (Means founder of Dispassion). Shiva Kaam Bhasmam (Destroyer of eroticism) makes you qualify to control your senses and nerves. The deity of eroticism (Kaam Dev) will not influence you.

- Om Namah Shivaya gives calmness to your mind Shiva holds moon crescent on his head. It impacts chanter body When somebody starts Om Namah Shivaya chanting. It cools his/her mind and helps them to get peace of mind, persistence, and calmness especially when everything is going against you.

- Om Namah Shivaya increases the happiness chemical which is known as GABA chemical. Lack of Gaba chemical reduces the natural sleep within humans. People who lack such chemical always feel exhausts. The frontal area of the human brain is in the Orbito prefrontal cortex which is responsible for making decisions, problem-solving and awakening the consciousness gets charged.

- Mantras bring you back to your source. Chanting or listening to mantras produce vibrations; positive, life uplifting energy, and are universal. Om Namah Shivaya is one of the most powerful mantras. Chanting this mantra builds the energy in your system and also clears the environment. People have been chanting this mantra for thousands of years.

- Om Namah Shivaya infuses positive energy and removes negative energy. It is also a stress-buster, helping you to relax and unwind.
- A restless mind becomes stable and peaceful with regular chanting.
- Om Namah Shivaya helps you to gain control over your senses. This will help you govern your mind eventually.
- Om Namah Shivaya gives you a sense of direction and purpose in life.
- There are nine planets and 27 constellations. Since the Shiva Tattva is the presiding energy and governs the planets as well, chanting Om Namah Shivaya can help nullify the effects of malefic planets to a certain extent.
- This mantra is associated with qualities of prayer, divine-love, grace, truth, and blissfulness. When done correctly, it allegedly calms the mind and brings spiritual insight and knowledge. It also keeps the devotee close to Shiva and within His protective global fellowship.
- Traditionally, it is accepted to be a powerful healing mantra beneficial for all physical and mental ailments. Soulful recitation of this mantra brings peace to the heart and joy to the Ātman or soul. Many Hindu teachers consider that the recitation of these syllables is

sound therapy for the body and nectar for the Ātman. The nature of the mantra is the calling upon the higher Self; it is the calling upon Shiva.

Details of Benefits of Chanting 'Om Namah Shivaya' Mantra will be discussed in the last chapter of this book.

CHAPTER 2

Maha Shiva Purana or Shiva Purana

2.1 About Shiva Maha Purana

Shiva Mahapurana as its name suggests is a holy text dedicated to and glorify Lord Shiva. Shiva Maha Purana had 12 Samhitas (chapters) and one Lakh (100000) shlokas in its original form; but a great number of its shlokas were lost and we are now left with seven chapters and 24,000 shlokas. The 5 lost chapters, the reference of which is found in other puranas are: Vinayaka Samhita, Maitri Samhita, Rudraikadasha Samhita, Sahasrakotirudra Samhita, and Dharma Samhita.

In Sanatana Dharma, Lord Shiva is worshiped as the first or the primordial man. Besides, in the initial section of the Brihadharma Purana, Shiva has been considered the creator, maintainer and destroyer of the entire universe. Well, we worship Shiva as a recluse and God but don't look into his other aspects. According to Shiva Purana, Shiva is also a true lover and a devotee. Let us consider all the aspects of Shiva as per the glory of Shiva described in Shiva Purana.

Who Is Shiva according To Shiva Purana?

This verse from the Brihadharma Purana will help us to understand the original form of Shiva:

Harihary o: Prakritireka Pratyabheden Rupbhedojyam.
Ekasyev Natsyanek Vidhe Bhed Bhedat.

Meaning: According to the above verse – there is basically no difference between Hari and Hara. The only difference is in their form. Just as an actor assumes different forms in a play, but in reality he/she remains who he/she is. This gives us an idea of the vastness of Shiva. According to Maha Shiva Purana, various things like yagya the time cycles of past, present, future and the entire world is created by the game of Lord Shiva, and he is seated in the midst of his creation.

The Shiva Purana composed by the Sage Veda Vyas is a great book describing the devotion and glory of Shiva. There are seven parts (chapters) in Shiva Maha Purana, in which various forms of Mahadeva (Lord Shiva) are described. Who are you Shiva from the stories of Shiva Purana by Veda Vyas? Or what is Shiva? You can know the answer to questions like these. We can use the teachings of Shiva Purana to improve our life and fill it with good qualities and live happily. Shiva Maha Purana serves to reveal to us the mysteries of Mahadeva, whose answers can change the way we see and live our lives. According to Shiva Purana, when you know about Shiva, you will find your own spiritual knowledge smaller. According to Shiva Purana, the worship method of Lord Shiva and his mantras work to bring us closer to the Lord. There is also a mention of stories related to the supreme devotees of Lord Shiva in the Maha Shiva Purana. Overall, through Shiva

Purana we can see that form of Lord Shiva which is unseen or untold for us till date.

In the Introduction to Shiva Purana, Sage Shaunaka expresses his desire to Sage Suta Mahamuni about knowing the stories about Shiva that could cleanse the mind and help him to attain Moksha. Suta, a disciple of Vyasa then narrated Shiva Maha Puranam which was originally told by Lord Siva to Brahma. Brahma taught the same to Sanath kumara and Narada; from them the great Vyasa learned this particular Purana and compiled as Shiva Maha Purana. The first seven chapters of Shiva Mahapurana recite the stories of Shiva Mahatmya and the benefits of listening and chanting Shiva Katha and how to get the best out of it. The stories related to Shiva are told in the subsequent chapters. **'OM Nama Shivaya'**, the Shiva Panchakshari Mantra (Penta syllable Ode) are revealed in this compilation of Purana.

As described in the earlier chapter, 'Om Namah Shivaya' (without 'Om') consists of the five letters Na, Ma, Shi, Va, Ya, or and. Thus, is called Shiva Panchakshari Mantra. These are the five holy letters which are most important while worshiping Shiva. 'Na' is the Lord's concealing grace, 'Ma' is the world, 'Shi' stands for Shivam (auspiciousness), 'Va' is His revealing grace, 'Ya' is the soul. Shiva Panchakshari Mantra is also taken as derived from Panchabhuta Tattva, the five seeds of the aforesaid natural elements. 'Na' consecrates Prithvi Tattva (Earth as matter), 'Ma' does the same with Jal Tattva (Water element), 'Shi' stands for Agni Tattva (Fire element), 'Va' stands for Vayu Tattva (Air element) and finally, 'Ya' stands for Akash Tattva (Sky element). Meaning of the word is: "Salutation to the Auspicious One or the Auspicious One exists in me".

According to Shiva Purana, Shiva or Maheshvara is the creator of Maya. That is, the Supreme Lord Shiva is beyond everything. He is immaculate, omniscient, above the three modes of nature and the ultimate Supreme Brahman. He is unborn and he is the origin of all. He is worthy of all the praise and is the guardian of his subjects, the god of the gods and worshipped by the entire world. According to Shiva Purana, Shiva is the sustainer and destroyer of the universe, he is the saguna-nirguna and the 'Nirvicāra Parabrahman Paramatma' in the form of true and divine nature.

According to Shiva Purana, Shiva himself tells Lord Vishnu, "O Vishnu, I am the source of creation, protection and destruction of the universe. I am the cosmic work divided into Trimurti and I am present in three forms and hold together Brahma and Vishnu." According to Shiva Purana, Shiva is anywhere and everywhere, so there is no point in asking who is Shiva? Or what is Shiva? Or where is Shiva? All this is just the result of limited thinking of our narrow thoughts. Shiva has just taken a form to be accessible to humans. Indeed, Shiva is omnipresent, omniscient and omnipotent.

2.2 Story of 'Om Namah Shivaya" in Shiva Maha Purana

Sage Shaunak expressed his desire to Sutji about knowing the means, which could help a man in this era of Kali (Kaliyuga) to attainment of Lord Shiva, by cleansing all the impurities of his mind and rectifying his inherent demonic tendencies. Sutji then described about Shiva Maha Purana- the supreme of all the puranas, which was narrated by Lord Shiva himself and which was later on retold by Sage Veda Vyas with the permission of

Maharshi Sanatkumar, for the benediction of common man. Sutji said, "By understanding the mysteries of Shiva Maha Purana and singing its praises, a man attains greater virtues than that which could be attained by being charitable or by the performance of all the `yagyas'. Contemplating on the subject matters of Shiva Maha Purana gives auspicious fruits just like a 'Kalpa-taru' (A mythological tree which fulfils all the wishes). Shiva Maha Purana contains twenty-four thousand shlokas. Shiva Maha Purana is the best means for man's liberation.

2.3 Proper Method of Listening to Shiva Maha Purana

Sage Shaunak requested Sutji to tell about the proper method of listening to Shiva Maha Purana, so that the mankind gets complete benefit. Sutji replied-

"First of all, an auspicious moment should be determined by an Astrologer. After that, friends and relatives should be invited, especially those who have the tendency of being away from such occasions. The sages and the virtuous people should be invited too. The 'Katha' must be held in scared places like Shiva temple, any place of pilgrimage or in one's home after doing a Bhumi Puja of the land where one intends to hold the Katha of Shiva Maha Purana. The canopy should be well decorated." "After making a resolution and doing worship of Ganapati - the destroyer of all hurdles and obstacles the Katha should be commenced. The person who is telling the 'Katha' should be facing the north and all the listeners should sit facing the east. The person who is telling the 'Katha' should be a scholar and should be capable of clearing all the doubts from the listener's mind. There should be no kind of distraction during the 'Katha' period. A devotee, who listens to the Katha, leaving behind all of his worldly worries, gets complete benefits. A devotee should also make donations and offerings according to his capacity and capability otherwise he would become a wretched man. The Mantra **'OM NAMAH SHIVAYA'** should be chanted throughout the period of Katha.

2.4 Rituals of Shiva Worship

On the request of the sages, Sutji describes about the methods of worshipping Shiva Linga. He says:

"One should construct a Shivalinga either of mud, rock or metal and establish it in such a place where it can be worshipped daily without any hindrance."

"The 'Char' (mobile) Linga should be small in size and the Sthira (Fixed) linga should be large. The Linga should be constructed along with the pedestal. The rule for constructing a Shiva Linga has been specifically described. The breadth of thickness of the Linga should be twelve times the thickness of the devotee's (one who is constructing the linga) finger, while the length should be twenty-five times. After establishing the linga in the above-mentioned way, it should be worshipped after performing the Shodasopachar. The thumb also symbolises a Shiva linga and its worship can be done. While worshipping the Shiva Linga, the mantra **OM NAMAH SHIVAYA** should be continuously chanted. Chanting this mantra for five crore times, helps a man in attaining to the abode of Shiva. Worship of Shiva done during the midnight is considered to be especially fructifying.

2.5 The Majesty of Pranav Panchakshara

The root sounds Akar, Ukaar, Makaar, Bindu and Naad, which are free from the delusions and which originates from the mother Nature are called Pranav. It is of two types:

a) Gross, b) Subtle. (Pranav Mantra OM AND **OM NAMAH SHIVAYA**).

2.6 Worship of Parthiva Linga

Sutji then explains the greatness of worshipping a Parthiva Linga:

"Parthiva Linga is the most the supreme among all the Shiva-Lingas. All the aspirations of the deities as well as men are fulfilled by the worship of Parthiv linga. During the era of Satya, jewel was considered to be of prime importance, whereas during Tretayuga and Dwaparyuga, gold and mercury had the prime importance respectively. In the present era of Kali, a Parthiva Linga holds this place of honour. The worship of Parthiva Linga begets more virtues than even penance. Just as Ganga among the rivers, Kashi among the sacred places of pilgrimages, Omkar among all the mantras are considered to be superior; in the same way Parthiva linga is considered to the supreme among all the Linga. Worshipping, a Parthiva linga with a 'Nishkama bhava' helps a man to attain liberation."

2.7 Methods of Worshipping Parthiva Linga

This Purana elaborately describes about the methods of doing worship of Parthiva Linga:

"After becoming fresh in the morning, a man should wear a rudraksha garland in his neck and apply bhasma (Ash) on his forehead. He should then worship the Parthiva Linga. He should chant the various names of Shiva, while worshipping the Parthiva Linga, like Har, Maheshwar, Shambhu, Shoolpani, Mahadev, etc. After worshipping the Parthiva Linga, it should be immersed in the river, Then the mantra - **OM NAMAH SHIVAYA** should be chanted with complete devotion. This is the method which has been described in the Vedas for the worship of Parthiva Linga."

2.8 Shabda-Brahma Tanu

We see all the vowels and consonants emanating from the physique of Mahadeva. Vishnuji saw the forty eight letters within OMKAR, which, in fact, were the two following mantras- "TATPURUSHAY VIDDYAMAHE MAHADEVAY DHIMAHI, TANNO RUDRAH PRACHODAYAT." And "TATSAVITURVARENYAM BHARGO DEVASYA DHIMAHI DHIYO YONAH PRACHODAYAT."

"After that we also receive the Mahamrityunjaya mantras like 'OM JOOM SAH", "HRAUM HRIM JOOM SAH" and "TRAYAMBAKAM YAJAMAHE". After that we receive the five lettered mantra **"OM NAMAH SHIVAYA"**, the Chintamani mantra 'KSHAMYAUM', the Dakshinamurti mantra - "OM NAMO BHAGAWATE DAKSHINAMURTAYE MAHYAM MEGHAM PRAYACHCHHA SWAHA. At last we receive the great mantra TATVAMASI. Vishnuji was so enchanted by this mantra that he started chanting this mantra. He then prayed to Shiva-the creator, the nurturer and the destroyer.

2.9 Story of Sandhya's Penance

Sandhya was very ashamed of herself. For the atonement of her sin she decided to do penance. She went to Chandrabhaga mountain and commenced her tremendous penance.

Lord Brahma then instructed Vashishtha to go to her in disguise and help in getting her initiated. He went to Chandrabhaga mountain in the guise of a brahmin and gave the mantra - **OM NAMAH SHANKARAYA OM** to her and also told her the methods of doing worship, then he returned back.

2.10 Narada Preaches Parvati

When Parvati reached her home, she became very sad as she was unable to bear the sorrow of Shiva's separation. Sage Narada arrived there. Her father Himalaya narrated the whole story to him

Sage Narada then gave the five lettered mantra – **'OM NAMAH SHIVAYA'** to her and he also instructed her to do penance. Parvati's heart was filled up with new enthusiasm.

2.11 Parvati Does Penance

After taking the permission of her parents and relinquishing all of her ornaments and royal apparels, Parvati went to the same place where Lord Shiva himself had done the penance. This sacred place was situated at the Himalayas, from where the holy Ganges originated. Parvati's companions too had accompanied her.

Parvati commenced her penance which gradually became severer day by day. She did penance for three thousand years by chanting the five lettered mantra- **OM NAMAH SHIVAYA** and performing other kinds of austerities. Becoming impressed by her tremendous penance even the deities flocked to see her. Parvati did her penance, surrounded by fire on all her sides during summer. In rainy season she did her penance without any shelter and during winter she used to do penance by immersing herself in neck deep water.

Initially lord Vishnu showed his disinclination to disturb Shiva's marital bliss, but when the deities insisted he went to Shiva accompanied by all of them. All of them eulogised Shiva and Parvati. The deities then requested Shiva to make his contribution in the destruction of Tarakasura.

2.12 The Deities Eulogize Lord Shiva

When the deities saw that the Tripurasura had become irreligious completely, they went to lord Shiva and requested him to kill Tripurasura. Right then mother Parvati arrived there accompanied by Kartik and Ganesha. She requested Shiva to come along with her into the palace. All the deities followed them and kept on requesting. The deities were angry that Parvati had caused obstacles in the fulfilment of their objective. They could not conceal their anger and expressed it.

One of the ganas of Shiva, whose name was Kumbhodar angrily attacked the deities. All of them got injured and went to lord Vishnu. Lord Vishnu advised them to chant the five lettered mantra - **OM NAMAH SHIVAYA** for one crore times. The deities followed the instruction. Lord Shiva became pleased and appeared before them. He assured the deities that their wishes would be fulfilled.

2.13 Lord Shiva Appears in the Guise of Indra (Sureshwar)

Upamanyu –the son of sage Vyaghrapaad, was brought up in his maternal uncle's home since his childhood. One day Upamanyu was very hungry. His mother gave him milk to drink which was not enough to satisfy his hunger. He demanded more and started crying. His mother mined some wheat flour in the water and gave him to drink as there was no milk left in the house. Upamanyu, finding the taste different, told his mother that it was not milk but something else. He again started crying.

His mother told him that if he wanted milk then he should worship lord Shiva as he only was capable of making the milk available. Upamanyu proceeded towards the Himalaya and started doing penance to please lord Shiva- continuously chanting the mantra **Om Namah Shivaya**. His penance generated so much of heat that all the three worlds started burning.

To test his devotion, Lord Shiva and goddess Parvati appeared before him disguised as Indra and Indrani respectively. Both of them told Upamanyu to stop doing penance. They said-

"We Indra and Indrani are extremely pleased by your devotion. Stop worshipping Shiva. We will fulfil all your desires."

Lord Shiva and goddess Parvati did not stop at this. They even cursed Shiva. Upamanyu became very furious and got up to attack the abuser – Indra.

Shiva and Parvati were satisfied by his total dedication and devotion. They revealed their real identity and blessed him.

Shiva promised Upamanyu that he would be present in the vicinity of his hermitage along with Parvati forever.

Upamanyu returned back to his home and narrated the whole story to his mother who was very pleased. Lord Shiva got the name 'Sureshwar' because he appeared in the guise of Indra.

2.14 Origin of Bheema Shankar

Bheema - the demon, was the son of Kumbhakarna and Karkati. After Kumbhakarna was killed by Sri Rama. Karkati and Bheema went to live at Sahya mountain.

When Bheema grew up he asked Karkati about his father. Karkati told him that his father had been killed by Rama. Bheema swore to avenge his father's death. He did a tremendous penance to please lord Brahma. Brahma appeared before him and blessed him with insurmountable power and strength.

Bheema then drove out the deities from heaven. He went to Kamarupa and defeated the king. He captured the king and put him in prison. The helpless king used to pass his time by chanting the mantra- **Om Namah Shivaya.** His wife worshipped the Parthiva linga of Shiva for the release of the king.

All the deities went at the bank of river Mahakashi and worshipped the Parthiva linga of lord Shiva. Lord Shiva appeared before them and assured them that the end of Bheema was near.

Lord Shiva went to the king who had been held captive by Bheema. His ganas too accompanied him. All of them waited for the opportune time to kill Bheema.

Meanwhile somebody informed Bheema that the king was doing worship of Shiva in the prison, with the objective of getting Bheema killed. Bheema arrived at the spot in the prison where the king was worshipping the Parthiva linga of Lord Shiva. He made fun of Shiva and struck the Shiva linga with his sword.

Right then, Lord Shiva appeared. A tremendous battle was fought between both of them. The battle continued for a long period. Sage Narada requested lord Shiva to kill Bheema as soon as it was possible.

Lord Shiva produced fire by his loud roar. In a very short time the fire spread in the whole forest. All the demons including Bheema were burnt to death. The deities and the sages arrived there. They requested Lord Shiva to remain there. Lord Shiva accepted their request and established himself in the form of Bheema Shankar Jyotirlinga.

2.15 Sri Krishna Does Penance

Sri Krishna proceeded to do his penance after getting initiated by Upamanyu with the mantra - **Om Namah Shivaya.** He did a tremendous penance for fifteen months by standing on his toe. In the sixteenth month lord Shiva and Parvati appeared before him after being pleased by his penance. Lord Shiva expressed his desire to bless Krishna. Krishna demanded eight boons: 1) May his intelligence always remain inclined towards religiousness. 2) May he attain immortal fame, 3) May he have his abode in Shiva's proximity, 4) May his faith and devotion in Shiva be unswerving, 5) May he have ten valiant sons, 6) May he be victorious against his enemies, 7) May all his enemies be destroyed and 8) May he be dear to all the yogis. After receiving eight boons from Lord Shiva, Krishna demanded one boon from goddess Parvati. May he always be in the service of his parents and the brahmins. Sri Krishna then went back to Upamanyu and narrated the whole story. At last he returned to Dwarka.

A brahmin should never have food during the night and should contently chant the **'Om Namah Shivaya' mantra.** Lord Shiva is not pleased that much by rituals as by faith and devotion. A man who worships lord Shiva while maintaining the rules of 'Varnashram Dharma', has the blessings of lord Shiva and all of his desires are fulfilled. If the devotee feels that something was lacking in the worship, he should atone for that mistake by chanting the Panchakshara mantra **Om Namah Shivaya.**

2.16 Seven Chapters of Shiva Maha Purana

The Shiva Maha Purana is divided into the following **Seven Samhitas** (Cantos).

(i) Vageshwari Samhita, (ii) Rudra Samhita, (iii) Shatrudra Samhita, (iv) Kotirudra Samhita, (v) Uma Samhita, (vi) Kailash Samhita, and (vii) Vayaviya Samhita.

Contents of each of these seven Samhitas are given below:

2.16.1 Vageshwari Samhita

Shaunkadi Muni's request. The greatness of Shiva Maha Purana. Final destiny path and the seeker. Liberation, thinking meditation and listening. Secrets of Shiv ling and the statue. The interaction between Brahma and Vishnu. Honesty of Vishnu honoured. Mercy on Brahma and a Kevda flower by Shiva. Practices in Shiva pooja and Maha Shivaratri. Pranav mantra advised to Brahma and Vishnu by Lord Shiva. Establishment of Shiva Ling and methods of worship and its benefits. Places of Shiva pilgrimage and specialty of each place. Daily religious duties (nithya karma) and duties of a person in grahastha ashram. The five mahayagna's with the principals and practices. Significance of area of donations and various vessels used in pooja. Parthiv pooja of Lord Shiva. Explanation on OM and Shiva ling worship methodology. The pictures of salvation and liberation and the methods of its achievements. Specialties of Shiva ling and Lord Shiva's worship. The Vedanta methodology of Parthiv Shiva ling prayers. Types and numbers of Parthiv Shiva ling, the methods and benefits of pooja vidhi. Sacrifices to Lord Shiva, (naivaidya) and pooja with Bili-patra. The powers and significance of bhasma (the holy ash), Bili and Rudraksha. The greatness of bhasma and its benefits. Rudraksha-its glory.

Shiva Purana Chapter 1 is known as Vidyeshwara Samhita. In the Vidyeshwara Samhita, the rules of reading the Shiva Purana, the rules of Shiva worship, the rules of Shivaratri fasting and the rules of worshiping Shivalinga, including the rules for wearing Rudraksha and the charity related to Shiva and their importance are found. It is stated in this chapter that Sutji is contemplating religion with the sages at Prayag.

2.16.2 Rudra Samhita

2.16.2.1 Shushtiushakyan Kanda:

Description of tapa by Mardi. Desires of Mardi. Advices from Lord Vishnu to Mardi. Questions asked to Lord Brahma by Narada. Creation of Vishnu. Arguments between Vishnu and Brahma. Description of shabda of Brahma. Mahadev's appearance and description of Shivattva. Blessings of Mahadev and creation of Mahakala. Methods of Shiva pooja. The nirgun and sagun bhakthi of Lord Shiva. Methods of prayers to Lord Shiva. Different types of Shiva pooja. Description of the nature and creation that was produced by Brahma. Characters of Gunanidhi. Salvation of Gunanidhi. Friendship of Lord Shiva and Kuber. Description of Rudra incarnation.

2.16.2.2 Sathi Kanda:

The holy tale of Sathi. Appearance of Kamdev. Curse of Brahma to Kamdev and well wishes. Marriage of Kamdev with Rathidevi. Description of the character of Sandya. The Tapa of Sandya and Lord Shiva's blessing to her. Appearance of Sandya from fire in the form of Asundhini. Appearance of vasant from the breath of Brahma. Kamdev attempts to attract Lord Shiva and his failure. Vishnu's advice to Brahma. Appearance of Shivadevi and the blessing of Brahma. Blessing of Shivadevi to King Daksha. Creation of Dacha and the curse from Naradji. Birth of Sathi and her childhood. Sathi's Shiva worship. Requisition of Vishnu and Brahma to Lord Shiva. Blessings of Lord Shiva to Sathidevi. Kanyadan of Sathi by Daksha to Lord Shiva. Blessings of Lord Shiva to Brahma. Lilas of Sathi and Shiva. The test to Ram by Shani. Separation of Sathi. Enmity of Shiva with Daksha. Starting of Daksha's sacrifice and Dhadhichi's sabha tyag. Sathi's attendance in Daksha's sacrifice. Sathi's anger. The departure of Sathi (Sathi's deh tyag). Creation of Veerabharu and Lord Shiva's orders to him. Attack of Veerabharu. The bad omens at the site of sacrifice of Daksha. Vishnu scolds Daksha. Dialogues between Vishnu and Veerabhadra. The war between Vishnu and Veerabhadra and the destruction of the sacrifice ceremony of Daksha. Dialogues between Dadhichi and Navraj. War between Vishnu and Dadhichi. The worships and prayers done by devas to Lord Shiva. The remedies to the sorrows of Daksha and others. The correction of Daksha's sacrifice.

2.16.2.3 Parvathi kanda:

The creation of Maina and the story of its curse. The worship of Goddess Jagadamba by the Devas. The blessing and help to Devas by Jagadamba. The birth of Parvathi. The childhood deeds of Pathvathi. The dialogues between Narada and Himalaya. The description of dreams and short description of character of Lord Shiva. The creation of Mangala graha the Bhoum. The meeting and unification of Shiva and Himalaya. The dialogues between Shiva and Himalaya. The dialogues between Shiva and Parvathi regarding Sankya and Vedantha. The creation of Vajag and his penance. The birth, penance of Tharakasur. The remedies to the sorrows of Devas. The destruction of Kamdev. Vadva nal Charittra. The advices to Parvathi by Narada. The enormous penance of Parvathi. The effects of the tapa of Parvathi. The acceptance of Parvathi for marriage. The test for Parvathi. The test of Parvathi by Lord Shiva in the form of a Brahmachari. The appearance of Shiva in front of Parvathi. The visit of Lord Shiva to Himalaya's place in the disguise of a beggar. The visit of Sapthadevas's to Himalaya's place. The character of King Anaranya. The characters of Padma and Pipla.. The preparation of marriage between Shiva and Parvathi, The departure of Lord Shiva for marriage. The arrival of Shiva at the gate of the city of Himalaya. The reception of Shiva and meeting between Devas and Parvathi. The advices given by all to Maina and the difficulties in making her understand. The description of the fantastic form of Shiva. The kanyadan of Himalaya to Shiva. The religious ritual of mangal phera of Shiva and Parvathi and desires (moh) of Brahma. The insulting words of the Kshatriya's for Shiva. Re-creation of Kamdev as a result of the prayers of Rathidev. The duties of pathivratha (righteous wife). The journey of Shiva and Parvathi to Kailash.

2.16.2.4 Kumar kanda:

The birth of Karthik to Lord Shiva. The creation of Karthik near Nandkeshwar. Karthik crowned as Bhrahamand's (universe) in-charge. The special characters of Kumar. The attack of Karthik on Thatkasur. The war between deva's and Daithya's. The battle against Tharkasur by Indra, Vishnu and Veerbhadra. The killing of Tharkasur by Kumar Karthik. Killing of demons — Ban and Pralab and the description of victory of Kumar. The characters of Karthik and Shivadevi. The creation of Lord Ganesha. The argument between Ganesha and Shivgana. The description of war of Ganesha. The beheading of Ganesha. The recreation of Lord Ganesha. The rank of in-charge of ganas (the followers) to Shri Ganesha. The preparation for the marriage of Ganesha. The marriage of Lord Ganesha.

2.16.2.5 Udha kanda:

The blessing of Brahma to the three sons of Tharakasur. The prayers and chantings of deva's to Lord Shiva. Shiva stuti. The benefits of panchakar mantra used in the worship of Lord Shiva. The chariot and other preparations of equipments for war. The attack of Lord Shiva on Tripur. Jaldar's creation and his marriage. The war between Jaldhar and deva's. The war between Vishnu and Jaldhar. Dialoges between devrishi Narad and Jaldhar. The message of Jaldhar to 'surrender Parvathi' to Lord Shiva. The attack of Jaldhar on Kailash. The ferocious battle between Lord Shiva gan and demons. Battle between Lord Shiva and Jaldhar. The disruption of Vrundha's pathivrath (her sincerity towards her husband) and her deh tyag (death). The killing of Jaldhar. The worship of deva's. The worship of deva's and the destruction of Vishnu's moh (desires). Shakchud's creation. The penance and marriage of Shankchud. The regime of Shankchud and the description of his previous birth. The worship of god of gods Lord Shiva. The advises of Lord Shiva. The destruction of Shanchud's forces. The killing of Shankchud. The curse of Tulsi to Vishnu. The killing of Hiranyakashyap. The tough penance of Andak and his procurement of blessing from Bhrama and related events. Starting of the war and the dialogue of the messenger. The war of Andak and the procurement of the title of Swami to his followers. The event of Lord Shiva swallowing Shukra. The exit if Shukracharya. The life of gan (follower of Lord Shiva) to Andhak. The description of procurement of life and the knowledge of death to Shukrachaarya. Ushacharitra - the disruption of marriage of Lord Shiva and Parvathi. Ushacharitra. The courageous deeds of Anirudha, his arrest and his liberation. The war between Banasur and Rudra with Shri Krishna. The cutting of Banasur's hands and reduction in his pride. The killing of Gajasur. The killing of Dhudhimbinihad. The killing of Vidal and Utpal the demons.

2.16.3 Shatrudra Samhita

The description of five incarnations of Lord Shiva. The descriptions of eight statues of Lord Shiva. The Ardhanareshvar (half male and half female) incarnation of Lord Shiva. The nine incarnations from Mahamunishwar to Vrishab. The other 19 incarnations of Lord Shiva. Nandeshwar Avathar. The abhishek (holy bath) of Nandeshwar. Bhairava avatar. The other story of Bhairav. The characters of Nurshi. The depowerment of Nurshi's pride — The shalbha incarnation of Lord Shiva.

The ghruhu pathi incarnation of Lord Shiva. Continuation of ghruhu pathi's story. Continuation of ghruhu pathi's story. Agneshwar avathar of Lord Shiva. Mahakal and other 10 avathars. The other 11 incarnations. The characters of Durvasa. Hanuman's character. Mahesh avathar. Vrushesh avathar. Vrushesh avathar(cont). Piplad avathar. The description of charects of Piplad. Vaishyanath avathar. Brijeshwar avathar. Pathinath and Bhrama ansh avathar. Vishnu darshan avathar. Avdhutheshwar avathar. Bhikshuvaurya avathar. Sureshwar avathar. Jatil bhramachari avathar. Suntharkanat avathar. Sadu vesh Bhrama avathar. Ashvathama avathar. Kiratha avathar and questions related to it; along with the answers and advises of Rishi Ved Vyas. The event of Kirat avathar and description of Arjun's penance. The killing of Mukdaitya(a demon)in Kirat avathar. The dialoges between Arjun and Kirath avathar bheel. The blessings to Arjun in Kirat avathar. Twelve jyothir ling.

2.16.4 Kotirudra Samhita

The descriptions of greatness of jyotir linga and the uplinga in different regions. The penance of Anusuya and Atri muni. The greatness of Atreshwar Shiva. The greatness of Nandikeshwar and the holy feet of Bhrama. The greatness of Nandkeshwar Shiv ling. Mahabal mahathma. The salvation of Chandal. The greatness of Shiv linga from Chandrabal to Pashupathinath. The reason for the linga form of existence of Lord Shiva. The reasons for creation of Batook. The greatness of twelve jyotir linga and the creation Somnath jyotir linga. Silikajun jyotir ling creation. The creation of Mahakal jyotir ling. The greatness of Omkareshwar jyotir ling. The greatness of Kedareshwar jyotir linga. The greatness of Bhimeshwar jyotir linga and the troubles caused by Bhimasur. The greatness and creation of Bhimeshwar jyotir linga. The greatness of Kashivihwanath and the arrival of Rudra to kashi. The effects of Shri Trambakeshwar jyotir ling and effect on Gautam. The description of misbehavior against Gautam. The goodness of Gautam and continuation of greatness of Triambekeshwar. The purification of Gautam and punishment to his culprits. The greatness of Vaidya Nadeshwar jyotir linga. The greatness of Nageshwar jyotir linga and the troubles caused by demons in Dharuka. The greatness of Rameshwar jyotir linga. The greatness of Dhumeshwar jyotir linga and sudeha and sudharma with its disruption and benefits. The appearance of Shri Dhumeshwar jyotir linga. The greatness of Hareshwar jyotir linga — the procurement of sudarshan charka by Vishnu. Hareshwar mahima with Shiv Sahastranam. The benefits of Shiv Sahastranam stotra. The king's and Deva's were known to be the devotes of Lord Shiva. The specialities of Shivratri. The begining of Shivratri vrath. The history of Shivratri related to a bheel (tribe) Mukthinirupan. Mukthinirupan. The secrets of Sugun and Nirgun. Gyanrupan.

Chapter 4 of Shiva Purana is known as Kotirudrasamhita. In Kotirudrasamhita, the importance of the 12 Jyotirlingas of Shiva and complete information related to their worship method is found.

- The information about how the 12 Jyotirlingas originated, with the meanings of the 12 Jyotirlinga Stotrams, the verses of 12 Jyotirlinga, etc. are obtained only from the Kotirudrasamhita.
- The story of Kashi Vishwanath, the origin of Kashi Vishwanath Jyotirlinga, the origin of Kashi, the mantra of Kashi Vishwanath, the secrets of Kashi Vishwanath are found in the Kotirudrasamhita.

- Information like the story of Mallikarjuna Jyotirlinga, the meaning of Mallikarjuna and how to worship Mallikarjuna Jyotirlinga is also found in the Kotirudrasamhita part of Shiva Purana.
- The story of Mahakal Jyotirlinga, the meaning of Mahakal Jyotirlinga, the story of the birth of Mahakal is also mentioned in the Shiva Purana of Dev Vyas.
- The story related to the origin of all other Dwadash Jyotirlingas including Kedarnath Jyotirlinga, Bhimashankar Jyotirlinga, Tryambakeshvar Jyotirlinga, Okareshwar Jyotirlinga, Rameshwar Jyotirling, Ghushmeshwar Jyotirling, Nageshwar Jyotirling and Vaidyanath Jyotirlinga is also available to us from Kotirudra Samhita.

We can also find the mention of the story of Vishnu getting Sudarshan Chakra by worshiping Lord Shankar. In the Kotirudrasamhita, information about the sources, methods and benefits of Shiva Sahasranama read by Lord Vishnu for Shiva worship is also found. It also entitles the information about fasts and mantras to please Lord Shiva. Additionally, the method of Shivaratri fast and the glory of Shivaratri are also mentioned in the Kotirudrasamhita.

2.16.5 Uma Samhita

The dialogs between Shri Krishna and Upamanu. The advises of Upamanu. The greatness of Lord Shiva who helped in development of his devotees. The effects of maya of Shiva. The descriptions of mahapapa (greatest sins) in the world. The description of ketlak upatha. The paths leading to hell and the description of Yamadutha. The description of hell. The description of fire of the hell. The details of which punishment is given for which sin in hell. The singnificance of ana-dan (donation of food). The effects of water resources, tree plantation, truth and penance. The greatness 26 puranas. The significance of samanya dan (common donations). The story of bhramand and description of pathal-lok. The methodology to get betterment from naraklok (the hell). Description of Jambhudveep. The sayings of dharma (the righteous duty) and the greatness of name of Lord Shiva. The significance of death in a war and other great proverbs. The creation of the human body. The remedies to diseases and stages of development of the body with the description of impurities in the body. The description of characters of a female. The knowledge regarding time of death, signs of death, and methods to measure the total life of a person. The methods of warding off the death or the kāla. The methods of achieving Shiva and description of death. Details of chayapurush. Details of adi shrusti. Details of daksh shrushti. The creation of deva's. The description of the dynasty of Kashyap. The deatls of creations of Bhrama. Details of sarvamanavatram. Vivasan manantra description. The 9 sons heredity of vavisaan manu. The dynasty from Satyavrat to sagar sudha. Kings of the dynasty. Shradhakalp — containing the effects of pitru (the spirits and souls of ancestors). The ceation of pitru and the fate of seven hunters. The effects of pitru (the spirits and souls of ancestors). Types of vyas pooja. The description of origin of vyas. Durga's first form Mahakali's description. Killing of Mahishasur. Durgas third incarnation Mahasarvathi and killing of Dharma Lochan, Chand, Mund and Rakthabijasur. Killing of Shumb and Nishumb the demons. Uhsa padhubhav description. Sathakshi incarnation. The dhrayug form of Jagadamba.

Uma Samhita gives information about the fruits of devotion and worship of Lord Shiva. The Chapter 5 of Shiva Purana Uma samhita gives answers to questions related to sin and virtue. The detailed tale about the appearance of Mother Uma and the slaughter of Shumbha Nishumbh is also available from Shiv Purana.

Moreover, how should a person perform actions to attain heaven and all the measures related to charity, virtue, these various details are from Uma samhita.

Uma samhita also mentions measures to remove sins and repentance of mistakes. The knowledge of all the four measurable practices for attaining immortality by conquering death, such as Pranayama, meditation of fire in the middle of the brow, breathing through the mouth and touching the bell of the tongue with a twisted tongue, is also obtained from the Shiva Purana.

Not just limited to this, the story related to Goddess Uma, Mahalakshmi, Saraswati and Kali incarnation is also found in the fifth chapter of Shiv Purana in Hindi literature.

2.16.6 Kailash Samhita

The dialogs between Vyas and Shaunkadi. The mysticism of pranava. The answers of Lord Shiva regarding pranav. The behavior of a sanyasi.The procedures of sanyas mandal. The description of sanyas cader by Vyas. The methods of meditation and devotion of Lord Shiva. Avaran poooja. Pranav artha padathi. The arrival of Shiva again to Kashi. The description of Vam Dev Brahman. The descriptions of pooja for the sanyasis. The description of Shiva swaroop pranav. Upasana and murthivarnan. The details of Shivthatva the substance of Shiva. The advaithya knowledge of Shiva and description of shrushti. Sanyas saptha padathi — the methods and practices for sculpturer. The great sentences of shruthi and the yogpad methodology. The methods and rules for the sanyasi and his sthan (place). The future of sanyasi after his death and the religious rituals after his death. The Ekadashi Krithya of sanyasi. Dwadhasha krithya of sanyasi.

In Kailash Samhita, we get information about various rules of Shiva Bhakti. Before imbibing dispassion and getting absorbed in the devotion of Shiva, you get the knowledge of the rules to worship Shiva from the Kailas sanhita. Herein, information about the classical method of taking sannyas is also found. Kailàsh Samhita also mentions worship of Ganapati, element purification, worship about Savitri, etc.

2.16.7 Vayaviya Samhita

In the complete section of Vayu Samhita, we find questions and answers between Sutji, sages and Brahma or the Supreme Person. Responding to the sages, Brahma refers to Rudra (Lord Shiva) as the Supreme Person. Besides, we also get to see the hymns and sources of Ardhanarishvara and the story of the killing of Shumbh Nishumbha by Maa Durga in this section of Vayu Samhita.

2.16.7.1 Purva bhag

The sayings of Vidya avathar. The proposals from the munis regarding the best man in the world. The arrival of Vayu deva in Namisharanya. Explanation of Shiva thatva. The effects of kal. The calculation of kal and the life expectancy of the three deva gods. The protector and destroyer of nature. The description of the location and situation of the universe. The description of nature. Creation of Bhrahma and Vishnu. The description of appearance of Rudra. The chanting of Shiva. The description of mahashakthi. The stories of nature. The departure of sati's soul from the body. The creation and origin of Veerbhadra. A lesson to deva-dhaksha chari. The defeat of all deva's by Veerbhadra. The rush of deva's to the holy feet of Lord Shiva. Regarding devi Kali and devi Gauri. The salvation of Karvad and the greatness of feet of devi Gauri. Meeting of Gauri and Shiva. The description of bhasmathatva. The substance of vani and artha. The questions related to Shiva thathva. Ripnupadesh. The description of shreshta anushtan. The description of pashupath vrath as said in Atharvashiras Upanishad. The discripitiion of tapa of Upamanyu. The characters of Upamanyu and Shiva's happiness towards him.

2.16.7.2 Uttara bhag

What is pashupathi gyan and why Shiva is pashupathi. The presence of Shiva in every thing. Gaurishankar vibhuthi yog. Pashupathi thathva rithi yog. Shivathatva description. Incarnation of Vyas and shivathathva gyan. The yogavathar of Shiva. The description of devotion to Shiva. Shiva rithi varnan. Powers of pachakshar mantra. The dikshavidhan (the method of learning) and gurumahathamya (significance of a teacher). Silpa sanskar varnan (the practices regarding statue creation). Shiva diva vidhan. Six track shudhi related stories. Importance of sanskar and mantra. Daily religious rituals. Daily regular karma(deeds) vrna(description). Pooja vidhan. The shtrokthi poooja varnan. Sanghopak pooja vidhi. Shiva shatroktha pooja vihdi. Agnikarya valan. Naithik vidhi karma. Kamaya karma varna. Shiva bhakthas kamya karma varnan. Kamya karma varnan in heaven. Description of Shiva maha stotra. Linga pooja secrets. Disruption of moh of Lord Bhrama and Vishnu. Solution of moh of Bhrama and Vishnu. Prathishta vidhi description. Yog vidhi varnan. The obstacles in the path of young. The description of Shiva yagna. Naimaishavarnan vasi rishi muni's journey details. Importance of Shiva Mahapuarn.

In this section of the Vayu Samhita, Vayudeva answers the questions of Sutji and other sages. In Shiv Puran Part 7 Vayu Samhita Uttara Khanda, Upamanyudwara Shri Krishna gets a description of the Pashupata weapon.

Herein, there is also a description of the omnipresence of mother Shiva's Uma Brahma form. Information related to Shiva's fasting, offerings and Havan Yagya are also seen in this section of Shiva Purana.

2.17 'Om Namah Shivaya' in "Shiva Purana'

2.17.1 Chapter Four

23-25. He shall repeat the mantra beginning with "Isana" and ending with "Sadya." After applying the ashes he shall repeat Om touching all the parts of the body. He shall wash his hands, feet and take the other ball. Adoring as before he shall apply three parallel lines on the forehead repeating the mantra 'Tryayusa' and the 'Tryambaka'. He shall apply the same on the chest with the Pranava and on the shoulders with "Om Namah Sivaya."

41. "Namah Sivaya", this mantra is directly expressive of Siva, the overlord of the gods, the bestower of boons.

42. The seven crores of mantras including the Pranava Om merge into this mantra and come out again.

43. Those Mantras are also beneficial with regard to those who are authorized therein. At the behest of the lord everyone is authorized in this Mantra.

44. Just as Shiva, this mantra too is capable of protecting all Atmans.

45. This mantra is **stronger than any other mantra**. Only this and no other mantra is capable of protecting all.

46. Hence eschew all the other Mantras and devote yourself to this **five-syllabled mantra**. When that is in the mouth nothing is inaccessible here.

47. The excellent Aghora missile affording protection to the devotees of Siva originates from this mantra. Considering this, be devoted to it and not otherwise.

48. This Bhasma produced in the Viraja fire was obtained by me from your father. It is excellent and it averts great mishaps.

49. Accept the Mantra bestowed on you by me. If the Japa of this mantra is performed your protection will be assured.

Vayu said: —

50-51. The mother directed him thus saying, "May it be auspicious" and allowed him to go. The sage accepted her words with his bent head. Bowing to her he made preparations for performing penance. Then the mother said to him (Upamanyu), "May the gods do everything auspicious for you."

52. Permitted by her he went to the mountain Himavat and performed penance with purity of minds. He took in only wind (no food).

53-54. With eight bricks he built an altar and installed Siva's phallic image of clay. He invoked the unchanging lord Siva accompanied by the Ganas and Parvati. He worshipped Him with the leaves and flowers available in the forest repeating the five-syllabled Mantra with devotion. He performed penance for a long time.

55-56. Assuming the forms of Rakshasa certain ghosts of sages cursed formerly by Marici harassed the lonely, lean boy Upamanyu performing penance though he was an excellent brahmin devotee of Siva. Thus they caused obstacles to his penance.

57. Though harassed by them he somehow maintained his penance. He uttered "Namah Sivaya" like one in great distress.

58. At the very hearing of that sound the sages who hindered the penance left off that boy and began to serve him.

2.17.2 Chapter Eleven

56. The Siddhis are achieved by the mantra, 'Om Namah Sivaya'. Hence the mantra shall be acquired for the acquisition of the great magnificence which has nothing parallel.

2.17.3 Chapter Twelve

Upamanyu said:

2. It is impossible to explain in detail the glory of the **five-syllabled mantra** even in hundreds of crores of years. Hence hear it in brief.

6. The omniscient lord Siva mentioned the mantra, "Om Namah Sivaya" for the acquisition of all topics and meanings by the embodied beings since it can be easily uttered through the mouth.

9-10. The five subtle Brahmans arc stationed in the mantra "Namah Sivaya" occupying one syllable each. Thus in the six-syllabled subtle mantra, Siva in the form of Pancha Brahmans is stationed in the way of Expressed and Expressive.

20. The Sivajnana, is as extensive as the expression of Siva, the six-syllabled mantra, 'Om Namah Sivaya'.

2.17.4 Chapter Thirteen

34. Of what avail are many mantras and Sastras full of details to one whose heart is firmly established in the mantra "Om Namah Sivaya?"

35. If anyone has stabilised the Mantra "Om Namah Sivaya" by frequent practice, he has learnt all, heard all and performed all.

36. Life is fruitful indeed, of the person, at the tip of whose tongue is present the sec of three syllables 'Sivaya' prefixed with the word denoting obeisance.

38. Now I mention the form of this great mantra. The word 'Namah' shall be uttered at first. It shall be followed by the word 'Sivaya'.

CHAPTER 3

'Om Namah Shivaya': Meaning and Significance

3.1 Significance of 'Om Namah Shivaya' Mantra

"Om Namah Shivaya"

Millions of people repeat mantras and say "Om Namah Shivaya" but they don't know the meaning. They don't even realize that they do not know what they are saying. They chant these Spiritual and Religious mantras for decades and generations, repeating the mantra without understanding its meaning. It actually means — "Om," a symbol of the Divine, "Namah," Namaskara or to bow down, and then the name of God. It means "O Divine! I bow down to you in the form of Shiva, "Om Namah Shivaya". We must stop praying without understanding what we are saying. Should we just pray or should ask and understand what we say to God? This is just one example of how we blindly follow myths and customs. It can be both useful as well as harmful. But each myth that was created was actually done so with a positive intention.

Many know this is the "Panchakshari" (5 letter) beeja or moola mantra for lord Shiva. "Shiv Panchakshari Mantra is drawn from the five elements of nature namely, Earth, Sky, Water, Air and Fire. This Mantra is capable of cleansing up all these elements. Seed of this Bija Mantra has all the characteristics of its parent body. In a way it is a miniscule of its parent form, complete with everything. A Seed of a gigantic banyan tree is a comparatively tiny object but it has everything in it, right from trunk, leaves and other attributes. Shiva Panchakshari Mantra is evolved from the five seeds of aforesaid natural elements, Namah Shivaya. Na Consecrates Prithvi Tattva, Ma does the same with Jal Tattva (Water factor) Shi energizes Agni Tattva (Fire element) Va energizes Vayu Tattva (Air factor) and finally Ya energizes Akash Tattva (Sky element). Om purifies Bramhatattva and Crown Chakra.

The importance and glory of this mantra is stressed across the Shaiva scriptures, as the most important mantra the devotee has to keep like own soul. Listing them would be highly arduous task given the importance this mantra gets in the scriptures. One may find a few of them in the stotras section and thirumurai medicine.

3.2 'Om' in 'Om Namah Shivaya'

3.2.1 Introduction

The first and the most important word in 'Om Namah Shivaya' Mantra is **'OM'** (or AUM): It is therefore imperative that a detailed description should be devoted to this sacred word 'OM' before we deal with the meaning and significance of this Mantra as a whole in the subsequent chapters.

Om is a sacred syllable representing Brahman, the impersonal Absolute, omnipotent, omnipresent, the source of all manifest existence. Brahman, in itself, is incomprehensible; so a symbol is used to help us realize the unknowable. Om is said to be the essence of all mantras, the highest of all mantras, the Divine Word or Shabda Brahman. It gives power to all mantras. Hence almost all mantras (like 'Om Namah Shivaya') begin with 'Om' and without it, mantras are said to be deprived of power. Om is the sound of the infinite. Om is said to be 'Adi Anadi', without beginning or the end and embracing all that exists. Om moves the *prana* or the cosmic vital force. Hence, it is called ***Pranava***.

The importance of Om is evident from the fact that Saint Dnyaneshwar, a renowned Indian saint who lived in the state of Maharashtra during the period 1275-1296, begins his Dnyaneshwari, a vernacular commentary on the Bhagavad Gita by addressing *Parmatman*, as *Om* and paying obeisance to Om. He says therein that the Vedas describe Om and conversely implies that the Vedas have emerged from Om.

In the linguistic sense, Om is a word from the Sanskrit language having its own root. It is derived from the root "*ava*" which is in the sense of *rakshanam*: protection, and also sustenance. Therefore, "ava - man" means the one who protects and sustains this entire creation (universe) by lending his existence and consciousness. By the rules of Sanskrit grammar, the suffix "man" in the word "ava - man" loses the last vowel, which gives "avam". Through vocalization process, "va" becomes "u", resulting in 'aum'. Further, "a" and "u" combine to form the diphtong, "O", finally yielding "Om".

Phonetic significance of Om: Every form of this creation (universe) is the God's form and the name for that form is the God's name. If the God is all, and one wants to give God a name, a name not in any particular language or alphabet, a name that is purely phonetic, that includes all the names that are there, what should one do? In any language, when a person opens the mouth and makes a sound without any other effort, it is "a". When one closes the mouth and makes a sound, it is "m". All other sounds in any language fall between "a" and" m". All the words in all languages are made up of letters, and the letters are, even if there is no script, are sounds. The one sound that represents all these sounds produced by the letters, is "a - u - m ", or "OM". It is the sound, which does not require the need of your tongue; so even a person who cannot speak (a dumb), even he can produce this great sound of OM, without any effort.

"Om it īdaṃ sarvam" (Taittirīya Upanishad 1.8) "This whole world is OM". The syllable OM, also known as Aum or Pranava, is the most sacred symbol of Hinduism, Buddhism, Jainism, Sikhism and Zoroastrianism. It is used both as a symbol and as a sound in religious worship, ritual chanting, performance of sacraments and rituals, meditation and tantra. In Hinduism, it is venerated as Brāhman ('Brahma Naada' or 'Pranava Nada'), in the form of syllable (Akshara) and sound (Shabda). Om is believed by many as "Apaurusheya" (not of human origin).

Initially, in the early Vedic period, because of the sanctity associated with it, the word 'OM' was kept as a secret and never uttered in public. It was used in private conversations and passed on from the teacher to the disciple or from father to the son directly and in secrecy. It was also not used in the rituals. Because it was not permitted to use the word directly, some early Upanishads referred to it indirectly as the udgita (upsound) or pranava (calling out), alluding to its significance in regulated breathing and religious chanting respectively.

The sacred OM is the primordial sound from which the whole creation has manifested. It is compared to the so-called scientific big bang theory. The Mandukya Upanishad deals with this topic in detail. The sound 'Om' is divided in four stages or parts. A.U.M. and the silence afterwards. These four represent the four states of human life, viz., the waking, dream, deep sleep and *turiya.* They also represent the three bodies, viz., Gross body, subtle body and causal body and the turiya or transcendental reality. *Turiya* is not a name but an indication for the self, which is the subtlest state or the transcendental meditation state in which, the body is completely at rest but the mind is fully alert (a state of 'restful alertness'). OM (AUM) is the mystic name for the Hindu Trimurti, and represents the union of the three gods: "A" for Brahma, "U" for Vishnu and "M" for Mahadev, which is another name of Shiva.

According to the science of mantra, there are four kinds of sound waves- standing waves, reverberant waves, oscillating waves, and transcendental waves. The mantra 'OM' produces all of these waves. Om is a combination of three sounds 'A', 'U' and 'M'. 'A' creates the standing wave, 'U' the reverberant wave, and 'M' the oscillating wave. The fourth wave, being transcendental and beyond the sense of hearing or speech, is created by meditating on Om in the heart centre. When we transcend the external sensory world, we become aware of high frequency waves, which have no rest period. Ordinary waves have a rest period. When we chant the mantra 'OM', it begins and it ends. The beginning and the end are the rest periods for the sound wave. However, when we transcend the mind, then we come to a high sound frequency, which has no rest period. The first three sound waves belong to the three dimensions of human consciousness and are interconnected. 'A' represents the waking or sense consciousness, 'U' the dream or sub-consciousness, and 'M' deep sleep or unconsciousness. The fourth wave represents the unlimited dimension of consciousness, which is beyond the mind and the senses. Therefore, we can say that Om has four bases: the sensual world, the mental world, the terrestrial world, and the ultimate state.

Various states of consciousness are illustrated in the following from the symbol of OM:

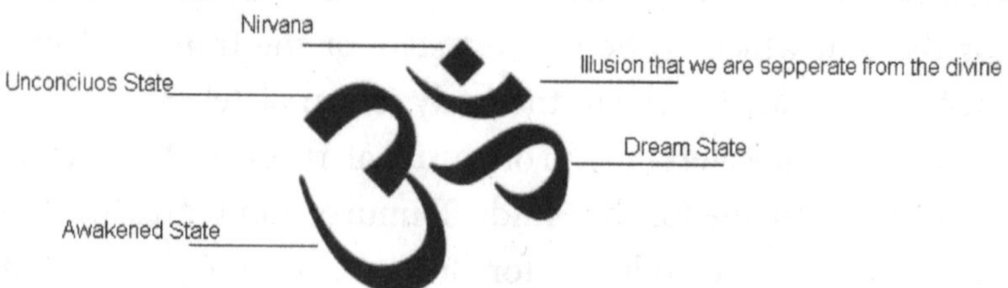

Decoding the symbol as written in Sanskrit brings deeper insight: the parts that resemble a "3" and an "o" represent three stages of the human mind's states of consciousness or progression from ignorance to clarity and the "cup shaped half circle" symbolizes that which separates these states from the "dot" which represents the true self.

Vaishvanara: the lower left curve (the bottom half of the "3") is the waking state, the conscious mind, which is focused outward to material objects and the gross or relative world.

Taijasa: (represented by the "o" to the right of the center of the "3") is the Dreaming state, active unconscious or the subtle world; that which is focused inward to only the thoughts in the mind.

Prajna: (represented by the top curve or upper part of the "3") is the casual plane of existence, the dreamless deep sleep state, deep meditation and latent unconsciousness.

Turiya: (represented as a dot or point above the top curve") the Bindu, absolute, pure unity consciousness, Atman/Brahman/Self. The "True Self" in its most un-worldly and purest consciousness (where) "*awareness of the world and of multiplicity is completely obliterated*". Turiya, "the true self", is separated from the other three states by a horizontal curve, the Naadi that means Sound; this is how Maya, the illusory world, the manifest or relative is transcended.

3.2.2 'OM' is Primordial

OM or AUM is not just a sound a vibration. It is not just a symbol. It is all that is within our perception and all that is beyond our perception. It is the core of our existence. OM was revered before the birth of all the religions in the world. The origin of "Big-Bang" is from the experiments made by Dr. Robert Wilson and Dr. Arno Penzias on microwave radiation in the universe. During their studies, they were continually getting some unknown radiation from the universe. This radiation was associated with the body at a temperature of 3^0 K and it is presumed that the radiation must have emanated when Big Bang took place.

Actually, their experiment proved the reverberation of the Big Bang explosion with which the universe began. Synonymous to this, our scriptures state that the sound OM or AUM – the Pranava mantra – was the first energy created at the time of disturbance of the equilibrium. It has been accepted in Hindu Religion that AUM, the first **primordial** sound energy ('Brahma

Naad') emerged in the process of creation. Hence, what the scientific experiments revealed as microwave reverberations during the Big Bang is already explicitly explained by our scriptures in the form of 'AUM'. "Om is the primordial throb of the universe. It is the sound form of Atman (Consciousness)." – Maitri Upanishad. According to Guru Granth Sahib, the most sacred book of Sikhs, The name of the Creator (OM or Ik Onkar) is True in The Primal Beginning. and True Throughout The Ages. (1-4, Japu, Mahalla 1)

3.2.3 'OM' is Apaurusheya

OM is the soundless sound of existence, which the Zen Buddhists refer to as 'the sound of one-hand clapping'. The sound of 'OM' is known as 'Anahata', which means un-struck sound. All the other ordinary sounds in the universe emerge as a result of frictional force between any two or more objects. Therefore, the 'OM' sound cannot be generated by person. It is self-producing sound. It is Apaurusheya. OM stands outside of history: as the distillation of the wisdom of the Vedas, the syllable remains "beyond human origin" (***apauruṣheya***), eternal, prior to everything (Pūrva Mīmāṃsā Sūtra 1.1.27-32).

3.2.4 'OM' is Perennial

OM is the akshara, which literally means immutable or imperishable, or perennial: the characteristic of the Syllable 'OM' as mentioned in the scriptures subsequent to Rig Veda. Therefore, OM is perennial, meaning that, it timeless, everlasting, which is valid in the past, present and future. As mentioned earlier, even Guru Granth Sahib mentions this to be perennial.

3.2.5 'OM' is Universal

OM is not related to any particular religion. As stated earlier, 'OM' is revered in many religions in the world: Hinduism, Buddhism, Jainism, Sikhism, and Zoroastrianism, to name a few. It is therefore 'Universal'.

3.2.6 Introduction to Ancient Hindu Texts

Before we refer to the mention of OM in the ancient Hindu texts, including Vedas, Upanishads, Smritis, Puranas, Bhagavad Gita etc, let us first briefly introduce these Hindu texts.

There are two historic classifications of Hindu texts: ***Shruti*** – that which is heard, and ***Smriti*** – that which is remembered.

The *Śhruti* refers to the body of most authoritative, ancient religious texts, believed to be eternal knowledge authored neither by human nor divine agent but transmitted by sages (*Rishis*). These comprise the central canon of Hinduism. It includes the **four Vedas** including its four types of embedded texts - **the Samhitas, the Brahmanas, the Aranyakas** and the early **Upanishads.** Of the *Shrutis* (Vedic corpus), the Upanishads alone are widely influential among Hindus, considered scriptures par excellence of Hinduism, and their central ideas have continued to influence its thoughts and traditions.

The ***Smriti*** texts are a specific body of Hindu texts attributed to an author, as a derivative work they are considered less authoritative than *Shruti* in Hinduism. The Smriti literature is a vast corpus of diverse texts, and includes but is not limited to Vedāngas, the Hindu epics, the Sutras and Shastras, the texts of Hindu philosophies, the Puranas, the Kāvya or poetical literature, the *Bhatia's*, and numerous *Nibandhas* (digests) covering politics, ethics, culture, arts and society.

3.2.6.1 The Vedas:

Veda means the supreme knowledge. The Vedas are a large body of Hindu texts originating in ancient India, with its Samhita and Brahmanas complete before about 800 BCE. Composed in Vedic Sanskrit, the texts constitute the oldest layer of Sanskrit literature and the oldest scriptures of Hinduism. Hindus consider the Vedas to be *apauruṣheya*, which means "not of a man, superhuman" and "impersonal, authorless". The knowledge in the Vedas are believed in Hinduism to be eternal, uncreated, neither authored by human nor by divine source, but seen, heard and transmitted by sages.

There are four Vedas: the Rig Veda, the Yajur Veda, the Sam Veda and the Atharva Veda.

i. **Rig Veda:** Some of the topics covered in this Veda are: Spiritual well-being and fulfilment, self-realization, peace of mind, Nirvana (Salvation), dutifulness, love, *Tapa,* compassion, human service etc. fall under the Rig Veda.

ii. **Yajur Veda:** Some of the topics covered in this Veda are: Generosity, valour, courage, gallantry, self-defence, leadership, fame, victory, power, dignity etc. fall under Yajur Veda.

iii. **Sam Veda:** Sam Veda deals with games, sports, amusement, recreation, music, arts, literature, sensual enjoyment, beauty, harmony, poetic imagery, dynamism, refined taste, gratification etc.

iv. **Atharva Veda:** Some of the topics covered in this Veda are: Wealth, prosperity, accumulation of money and resources, animals, medicines, food grains, materials, metals, buildings, vehicles and similar other materials of worldly being fall within the purview of Atharva Veda.

Rik is also known as righteousness (*Dharma*), Yajur as liberation (*Moksha*), Sam as sensual pleasure (*Kama*) and Atharva as prosperity (*Arth*). These are the four faces of Brahma.

Each Veda has been sub classified into four major text types – the Samhitas (mantras and benedictions), the Aranyakas (text on rituals, ceremonies, sacrifices and symbolic-sacrifices), the Brahmanas (commentaries on rituals, ceremonies and sacrifices), and the Upanishads (text discussing meditation, philosophy and spiritual knowledge).

3.2.6.2 The Upanishads:

Over a period that spanned between 2100 and 1900 B.C.E, Vedic knowledge was absorbed into a process of reinterpretation that included the Upanishads. This was esoteric knowledge and was gradually freed from sacrificial Vedic rituals. Characteristic of the Upanishads was an intimacy of instruction, an initiation which "suggested in the word itself "sitting down near" (upa "near", ni "down" shad "to sit"), that is, sitting down near the teacher. Upanishads are the philosophical culmination of the Vedic thoughts. Coming at the end of Vedas, the Upanishads are also referred to as Vedanta.

The Upanishads are a collection of Hindu texts, which contain some of the central philosophical concepts of Hinduism. The Upanishads are commonly referred to as *Vedānta*, variously interpreted to mean either the "last chapters, parts of the Veda" or "the object, the highest purpose of the Veda". The concepts of Brahman (Ultimate Reality) and Ātman (Soul, Self) are central ideas in all the Upanishads, and "Know your Ātman" their thematic focus. The Upanishads are the foundation of Hindu philosophical thought and its diverse traditions. Of the Vedic corpus, they alone are widely known, and the central ideas of the Upanishads have had a lasting influence on Hindu philosophy.

The exact number of the Upanishads is not clearly known. The original Upanishads are the end portions of the four Vedas, and thereby came to be identified with "Vedanta", which literally means the end of the Vedas. They dealt with the philosophical aspects of the Vedas and were taught in ancient India to highly qualified and selected individuals. Today there are estimated to be about 350 Upanishads, some well-known and some least known. The Bhagavad-Gita of Lord Krishna is also considered an Upanishad because it contains the essence of many of the Upanishads. The *mukhya* Upanishads are found mostly in the concluding part of the *Brahmanas* and *Aranyakas* and were, for centuries, memorized by each generation and passed down verbally. The early Upanishads all predate the Common Era, some in all likelihood pre-Buddhist (6th century BCE), down to the Maurya period. Of the remainder, some 95 Upanishads are part of the Muktika canon, composed from about the start of common era through medieval Hinduism. New Upanishads, beyond the 108 in the Muktika canon, continued to being composed through the early modern and modern era, though often dealing with subjects unconnected to Hinduism.

The Upanishadic texts are part of the Shruti literature and are considered to be divine in origin. They are associated with the names of several ancient seers. Some of these lived at least twenty generations before Lord Krishna and the probable date of the Mahabharata war. Prominent among these sages were Yajnavalkya, Uddalaka Aruni, Shandilya, Aitareya, Pipplapada and Sanatkumara.

As per the list contained in the Muktikopanishad, 108 Upanishads are given below. These are arranged in four categories according to the particular Veda to which each of them belong.

Vedas (No. of Associated Upanishads)	Associated Upanishads
Rig Veda (10)	Aitareya, Atmabodha, Kaushitaki, Mudgala, Nirvana, Nadabindu, Akshamaya, Tripura, Bahvruka, Saubhagyalakshmi.
Yajurveda (50)	Katha, Taittiriya, Isavasya, Brihadaranyaka, Akshi, Ekakshara, Garbha, Prnagnihotra, Svetasvatara, Sariraka, Sukarahasya, Skanda, Sarvasara, Adhyatma, Niralamba, Paingala, Mantrika, Muktika, Subala, Avadhuta, Katharudra, Brahma, Jabala, Turiyatita, Paramahamsa, Bhikshuka, Yajnavalkya, Satyayani, Amrtanada, Amrtabindu, Kshurika, Tejobindu, Dhyanabindu, Brahmavidya, Yogakundalini, Yogatattva, Yogasikha, Varaha, Advayataraka, Trisikhibrahmana, mandalabrahmana, Hamsa, Kalisantaraaa, Narayana, Tarasara, Kalagnirudra,Dakshinamurti,Pancabrahma, Rudrahrdaya, SarasvatIrahasya.

Continued...

SamaVeda (16)	Kena, Chandogya, Mahat, Maitrayani, Vajrasuci, Savitri, Aruneya, Kundika, Maitreyi, Samnyasa, Jabaladarsana, Yogachudamani, Avyakta, Vasudeva, Jabali, Rudrakshajabala.
Atharvaveda (32)	Prashna, Mandukya, Mundaka, Atman, Surya, Narada-Parivrajakas, Parabrahma, Paramahamsa-Parivrajakas, Pasupatha-Brahma, Mahavakya, Sandilya, Krishna, Garuda, Gopalatapani, Tripadavibhuti-mahnarayana, Dattatreya, Kaivalya, Nrsimhatapani, Ramatapani, Ramarahasya, HayagrIva, Atharvasikha, Atharvasira, Ganapati, Brhajjabala, Bhasmajabala, Sarabha, Annapurna, Tripuratapani, Devi, Bhavana, SIta.

3.2.6.3 Post-Vedic Texts

The texts that appeared afterwards were called Smriti. Smriti literature includes various Shastras and Itihasas (epics like Ramayana, Mahabharata), Harivamsa Puranas, Agamas and Darshanas. The Sutras and Shastras texts were compilations of technical or specialized knowledge in a defined area. The earliest are dated to latter half of the first millennium BCE. The Dharma shastras (law books) include derivatives of the Dharma-sutras. Other examples were Bhautikashastra (Physics), Rasayanashastra (Chemistry), Jīvashastra (Biology), Vastushastra (Architectural science), Shilpashastra (Science of sculpture), Arthashastra (Economics) and Nītishastra (political science) It also includes Tantras and Āgama_ (Hinduism) literature. This genre of texts includes the Sutras and Shastras of the six schools of Hindu philosophy.

3.2.6.4 The Bhagavad Gita

The Bhagavad Gita is a 700–verse Hindu scripture that is part of the ancient Sanskrit epic *Mahabharata*. This scripture contains a conversation between Pandava prince Arjuna and his guide Krishna on a variety of philosophical issues. Commentators see the setting of the Gita in a battlefield as an allegory for the ethical and moral struggles of the human life. The Bhagavad Gita›s call for selfless action inspired many leaders of the Indian independence movement including Mohandas Karamchand Gandhi, who referred to the Gita as his "spiritual dictionary". Numerous commentaries have been written on the Bhagavad Gita with widely differing views on the essentials, beginning with Shankara's commentary on the Gita in the 8th century CE.

3.2.6.5 The Smritis

The Smritis function as unwritten code of conduct. They lay down the norms of behaviour in the Society and also are advisory in Nature to kings and his subjects. Smritis also reflect the social Life of the Vedic India down the Ages. There are **Eighteen Smritis**. These are also called **Dharma Shastras**, Rules of Righteousness. They are: (1) Manu, (2) Yajnavalkya, (3) Parasara, (4) Vishnu, (5) Daksha, (6) Samvarta, (7) Vyasa, (8) Harita, (9) Satatapa, (10) Vasishtha, (11) Yama, (12) Apastamba, (13) Gautama, (14) Devala, (15) Sankha-Likhita, (16) Usana, (17)Atri and (18) Saunaka.

3.2.6.6 The Puranas

The Puranas are a vast genre of Hindu texts that encyclopaedically cover a wide range of topics, particularly myths, legends and other traditional lore. Composed primarily in Sanskrit, but also in regional languages, several of these texts are named after major Hindu deities such as Vishnu, Shiva and Devi.

a. **Major Puranas:** The following are the following 18 major puranas:

   (1) Brahma Purana, (2) Padma Purana, (3) Vishnu Purana, (4) Skanda Purana, (5) **Shiva Maha Purana**, (6) Vamana Purana, (7) Markandeya Purana, (8) Varaha Purana, (9) Brahma Vaivarta Purana, (10) Agni Purana, (11) Bhavishya Purana, (12) Matsya Purana, (13) Garuda Purana, (14) Brahmananda Purana, (15) Shrimad Bhagavat Purana, (16) Kurma Purana, (17) Linga Purana, (18) Narad Purana

b. **Minor Puranas:** The following are the following 18 minor puranas:

   (1) Sanatkumar purana, (2) Narasimha purana, (3) Brihannaradiya purana, (4) Sivarahasya purana, (5) Durvasa purana, (6) Kapila purana, (7) Kapila purana, (8) Bhargava purana, (9) Varuna purana, (10) Kalika purana, (11) Samba purana, (12) Nandi purana, (13) Surya purana, (14) Parasara purana, (15) Vashishtha purana, (16) Devi-Bhagvata purana, (17) Ganesha purana, and (18).Hamsa purana

3.2.7 'OM' in Hinduism

3.2.7.1 OM in Rig Veda

Significantly, the syllable *om* is not mentioned in the ancient *Rig-Veda,* which has recently been dated back to the third millennium B.C.E and earlier still. However, a veiled reference to it may be present in one of the hymns (1.164.39), which speaks of the syllable (*akshara*) that exists in the supreme space in which all the deities reside. "What," asks the composer of this hymn, "can one who does not know this do with the chant?" He adds, "Only those who know it sit together here." That is, only initiates gather to delight in the mystery of the sacred syllable and the company of the deities. The word *akshara* means literally "immutable" or "imperishable." This designation is most appropriate, since grammatically syllables are stable parts that make up words. In the case of the mantric *om,* this monosyllable came to represent the ultimate One, which is eternally unchanging (*akshara, acala*).

Richo akshare parame vyoman,
yasmin deva adhi vishve nishedhuhu|
Yasthannaveda kim richa karishyathi,
yayithath vidu stha ime samasathe||

– Rig Veda (1.164.39),

"Richa is situated in akshara. knowledge is structured in consciousness, the non-changing transcendental basis of all relative existence in which reside the impulses of creative intelligence responsible for the whole manifest universe. He whose awareness is not open to this level of reality, what can these eternal expressions of knowledge accomplish for him?"

OR, in other words:

"He who knows not the eternal Syllable (Akshara) of the Veda, the highest point upon which all the gods repose, what business has he with the Veda? Only its knowers sit here in peace and concord".

3.2.7.2 OM in Yajur Veda

As time went by, the ban on uttering the sacred syllable or even writing it down outside the sacrificial rituals was relaxed. Thus the sacred syllable is first mentioned by name in the opening hymn of the *Shukla-Yajur-Veda* (1.1), the "white" recession of the Vedic hymnody dealing strictly with the performance of the sacrifices (*yajus*). This could be a later addition, however. For the *Taittirîya-Samhitâ* (5.2.8), which is appended to the *Yajur-Veda*, still cryptically speaks of the "divine sign" (*deva-lakshana*) that is written threefold (*tryalikhita*).

Yajurveda (40.17) is also called Isha Upanishad. It says:

Om krato smara. Vayur-anilam-amrtam athedam
Bhasmantagm sariram,
Om krato smara krtagm smara, krato smara krtam smara.

O men, at the time of death remember OM, the name of God. Think about God and yourself, think about the deeds you performed in your entire life. The vayu takes the soul. And remember that the body is mortal and will be finally destroyed.

"O3m krato smara |"

'O3m' is the highest reality. Here, the number intervening between o and m refers to 3 aspects of 'om' – (1) the sound originating in muladhara, (2) proceeding toward chest and (3) entering and spreading in the head; it spreads in three vyahrti-bhu, bhuvah, and svah. Therefore 'OM' is also referred to as 'AUM', where 'A' represents Agni, 'U' represents Vayu, and 'M' represents Aditya.

3.2.7.3 OM in Aitareya-Brahmana

Om ityasau yo'sau [sûryah] tapati. Aitareya-Brâhmana (5.32)

"That which glows [that is, the Sun] is Om."

3.2.7.4 OM in Brihadaranyaka Upanishad

yō ha vai jyēṣṭhaṅ ca śrēṣṭhaṅ ca vēda jyēṣṭhaśca ha vai śrēṣṭhaśca bhavati prāṇō vāva jyēṣṭhaśca śrēṣṭhaśca || 5.1.1 ||

"Om is Brahman, the Primeval Being. This is the Veda which the knowers of Brahman know; through it one knows what is to be known".

3.2.7.5 OM in Chandogya Upanishad

ōmityētadakṣaramudgīthamupāsīta. ōmiti hyudgāyati tasyōpavyākhyānam (1.1.1)

"One should meditate on this syllable: Om. That is the quintessence of the essences, the Supreme, the highest" (Chandogya Upanishad 1.1.1).

Sa esha rasana rasatamah paramah paradhyorashtamo yadudgeethah. (1.1.3)

"The syllable OM, which is called Udgitha, is the quintessence (means the most perfect) of the essences, the supreme, deserving of the highest place." (Chandogya Upanishad 1.1.3)

This can be said, because Om is the Primal Word, the Original Sound, the First Word "spoken" by God, and by which all that "is" was created, and is being sustained and evolved at this very moment.

Tadetanmithunamomityetasminnaksharesagvung srijyate yada vai mithunau samagachchata aapayato vai tavanyonyasya kamam. (1.1.6)

"Speech and breath are joined together in the Syllable OM" (Chandogya Upanishad 1.1.6)

Omiyetadaksharamudgeethamupasitomiti hyudgayati tasyopavyakhyanam. (1.4.1)

"One should meditate on Om.... This sound is that syllable, the immortal, the fearless. having entered this, the gods become immortal, fearless. He, who knowing it thus, praises this syllable, take refuge in that syllable, in the immortal, fearless sound, and having entered it, he becomes immortal, even as the gods became immortal" (Chandogya Upanishad 1.4.1-5).

Athadhyatmam ya evayam mukhyah pranastmudgeethamupasitomiti hyesha svaranneti (1.5.3)

"The breath is continually sounding Om" (Chandogya Upanishad 1.5.3).

Sa esha parovariyanudgeethah sa eshonnatah parovariyo hasya bhavati parovariyaso ha likajjayati ya etadevam vidvanaparovariya samugeethamupaste. (1.9.2)

"This is the Udgitha (the song as OM, which uplifts the singer), the most excellent; this is endless. He who, knowing this, meditates on the Udgitha; obtsins progressively the most excellent life and wins the most outstanding worlds." (Chandogya Upanishad 1.9.2).

Agnihirkaro vayuha prastava aaditya udgeetho nakshatrani pratiharaschaandrama nidhanametadrajanamadevatasu pritam. (2.20.1)

"The sun is Om" (Chandogya Upanishad 2.20.1).

Tanyabhyatapattebhyobhitaptebhya omkarah samprasravattadyatha shadakuna sarvani paranani. Santrinnanyevamomkaren sarva vakasantrinnomkara eveda sarvamomkara eveda sarvam. (2.23.3)

"As all leaves are held together by a stalk, so is all speech held together by Om. Verily, the Syllable Om is all this" (Chandogya Upanishad 2.23.3).

Tadyatha aahapath aatata ubhau gramau gachchateemam chamum chaivamevaita aadityasya rashmay ubhau lokau gachchanteem chamum. Chamushmadadityatpratayante ta aasu nadishu sripta aabhyo nadibhyah pratayante teyamushminnadte sriptah. (8.6.2)

"Even as a great extending highway runs between two villages, this one and that yonder, even so the rays of the sun go to both these worlds, this one and that yonder. They start from the yonder sun and enter into the. They start from the naadis and enter into the yonder sun.... When a man departs from this body, then he goes upwards by these very rays or he goes up with the thought 'Om.' As his mind is failing, he goes to the sun. That, verily, is the gateway of the world, an entering in for the knowers, a shutting out for the non-knowers".

– (Chandogya Upanishad 8.6.2, 5).

3.2.7.6 OM in Katha Upanishad

Sarve Veda Yatpadmamananti tapasi sarvani cha yadvadanti.
Yadichchanto brahmacharyam charanti tatte pada sangrahen
braveemyomityetat. (15)

Etaddhyevaksharam Brahma etaddhyevaksharam param.
Etaddhyevaksharam gyatwa yo yadichchati tasya tat. (16)

Etadalambanam shreshthametadalamanam param.
Etadalambanam gyatwa brahmaloke maheeyate. (17)

"That word which all the Vedas declare, which all the austerities proclaim, desiring which people practice brahmacharya that word, to you I shall tell in brief: It is Om. This syllable is, verily, the everlasting Spirit. This syllable is, indeed is the highest end; knowing this very syllable, whatever anyone desires will be his. This support is the best. This support is the highest; knowing this support, one becomes great in the world of Brahma"

– (Katha Upanishad 1.2.15-17).

3.2.7.7 OM in Mandukya Upanishad

Om ityetadakshamida sarvam tasyopavyakhyanam.
Butam bhasva bhavishaditi sarvamomkar aiv.
Yachchanyat trikalateetam tadapyomkar aiv. (1)

Soayamatmadhyaksharamomkaro adhimitram pada
matrashcha pada
Akar ukaro makaar iti. (8)

Amatrashchturtho vyavahatyah pranchopeshamah shivo advait.
Evamomkar aatmaiva samvishatyatmanam ya evam veda. (12)

"Om: this syllable is all this.... All that is the past, the present and the future, all this is only the syllable Om. And whatever else there is beyond the threefold time, and that too is only the Syllable Om.... The Self is of the nature of the Syllable Om.... Thus the Syllable Om is the very Self. He who knows it thus enters the [Supreme] Self with his [individual] Self"

Om-ity-etad-aksharam-idam sarvam, tasyopavyakhyanam bhutam bhavad bhavishyaditi sarvam-omkara eva. Yaccanyat trikalatitam tadapy omkara eva.

– Mandukya Upanishad 1, 8, 12

All is OM: Hari Om. The whole universe is the syllable Om. Following is the exposition of Om. Everything that was, is, or will be is, in truth Om. All else which transcends time, space, and causation is also Om.

Soayamaymadhyakshamonkaroadhimatram pada matra matrashcha akaar ukaro makaar iti.

The Four states of consciousness are the Same as "A-U-M", followed by Silence: That Om, though described as having four states, is indivisible; it is pure Consciousness itself. That Consciousness is Om. The three sounds A-U-M (ah, ou, mm) and the three letters A, U, M are identical with the three states of waking, dreaming, and sleeping, and these three states are identical with the three sounds and letters. The fourth state, Turiya is to be realized only in the silence behind or beyond the other three.

Dhanur gṛhīvtā aupaniṣadam mahāstraṁ śaraṁ hy upāsā-niśitaṁ saṁdadhīta, āyamya tad-bhāvagatena cetasā lakṣyaṁ tad evākṣaraṁ, saumya viddhi (2.2.3).

"Taking as the bow the great weapon of the Upanishads [Om], one should place in it the arrow sharpened by meditation. Drawing it with a mind engaged in the contemplation of That [Brahman], O beloved, know that Imperishable Brahman as the target.

– (Mundaka Upanishad 2.2.3).

3.2.7.8 OM in Prashna Upanishad

Etadvai satyakaam param chaparam cha brahma yadonkarah.
Tasmadwidwanetenaivayatanainaikataramanveti. (5.2.2)

Yah punaretam trimatrenomityetenaivaksharen param purushamabhi dyayaeet sa tejasi surye sampannah. Yatha padodarastvacha vinirbhuchyat evam ha vai sa papmana vinibhuktah sa samabhirunneeyate brahmalokam sa etasmajjeevaghanat paratparam prushatam purushameekshate. Tadetau shlokau bhavatah. (5.2.5)

Rigbhiretam yajurbhirantariksham samabhiryata tat kavayo vedayante.
Tamonkarenaivayatanenanveti vidvan yattachchantamajaramamritamabhayam param cheti. (5.2.7)

"Satyakama, son of Shibi, asked [the Rishi Pippalada]: 'Venerable Sir, what world does he who meditates on the Omkara until the end of his life, win by That?' To him, he said: 'That which is the Omkara, O Satyakama, is verily the higher and the lower Brahman. Therefore, with this support alone does the wise man get one or the other.'... If he meditates on the Supreme Being [Parampurusha] with the Syllable Om, he becomes one with the light, the Sun. He is led to the world of Brahman. He sees the Person that dwells in the body, who is higher than the highest life.... That the wise one attains, even by the Omkara as a support, that which is tranquil, un-aging, immortal, fearless, and supreme"

– (Prashna Upanishad 5:2, 5, 7).

3.2.7.9 OM in Shvetashvatara Upanishad

Udgeetametatparam tu brahma tasmimstrayam supratishthaksharam cha.
Atrantaram brhmavido viditva leena brahmani tatpara yonimuktah.

– (Shvetashvatara Upanishad 1:7)

"Om has been sung as the supreme Brahman, and in it are the Triad [the individual spirit, the cosmos, and the Cosmic Spirit]. It is the firm support, the imperishable. The knowers of Brahman by knowing what is therein become merged in Brahman, intent thereon and freed from birth" (Shvetashvatara Upanishad 1:7).

Vahneryatha yonigstasya murtinar drishyate naiva cha linganashah.
Sa bhooya evendhanayonigrihya stadvobhayam vai pranaven dehe. (1.13)

Svadehamaranim kritva pranavam chottararanim.
Dhyananirmathanabhasadevam pashyannigoodhavat. (1.14)

"As the form of fire when latent in its source is not seen and yet its seed is not destroyed, but may be seized again and again in its source by means of the drill [a pointed stick whirled to produce fire for the Vedic sacrifices], so it is in both cases. The Self has to be seized in the body by the Pranava. By making one's body the lower friction stick and the Pranava the upper friction stick, by practicing the friction of meditation one may see the hidden God" (Shvetashvatara Upanishad 1:13, 14).

3.2.7.10 OM in Bhagavad Gita

Raso aham aapsu kauntuya prabhutva sasi suryaha pranava vedasu sabda hai paurasam nrasu. (7:8)

"O son of Kuntī, I am the taste of water, the light of the sun and the moon, the syllable Pranava (OM) in the Vedic mantras; I am the sound in ether and ability in man. " (Bhagavad Gita 7:8).

Omityekaksharam Brahma vyaharanmamanusmaran.
Yah prayati tyajandeham sa yati paramaam gatim. (8:13)

"Uttering Om, the single-syllabled Brahman, meditating on me, departing thus from his body, he attains the Goal Supreme" (Bhagavad Gita 8:13).

Pitahamasya jagato mata dhata pitamahah.
Vedyam pavitramonkar riksaam yajureva cha. (9.17)

"I am the father of this universe, the mother, the support, and the grandsire. I am the object of knowledge, the purifier and the syllable om. I am also the Rig, the Sama, and the Yajur [Vedas]." (Bhagavad Gita 9:17).

Maharishinaam Bhriguraham Giramasmyekamaksharam.
Yagyanaam japayagyosmi sthavarannam himalayah. (10.25)

"Of the great sages I am Bhrigu; of vibrations I am the transcendental om. Of sacrifices I am the chanting of the holy names [japa], and of immovable things I am the Himalayas." (Bhagavad Gita 10:25).

Tasmaad Om iti udrahit yagya-dana-tapa-kriyaha.
Pravartak vidonokat satatma Brahma-vaadinam. (17:24)

Thus the transcendentalists undertake sacrifices, charities, and penances, beginning always with OM, to attain the Supreme. (17:24)

3.2.7.11 OM in Manu Smriti

The Laws of Manu (Manu Smriti) is the oldest code of laws in India.

Ekaksharam param Brahma pranayamah param tapah.
Saavitryastu param nasty maunatsatyam vishishyate.

– Manu Smriti, 2.83

"The monosyllable Om is the highest Brahman. … Undoubtedly a Brahmin reaches the highest goal by japa of Om alone, whether he performs other rites or neglects them" (Manu Smriti 2:83, 87).

3.2.7.12 OM in Mandukya Karika

Omkaram padasho vidyatpada matra na sanshayah.
Omkaram padasho gyatva na kinchidapi chintayet.

– Mandukya Karika, (1.24)

"Om should be known. Having known Om, one should not think of anything whatsoever" (Mandukya Karika 1:24).

Yunjeet pranave cheetah pranavo brahma nirbhayam.
Pranave nityktasya na bhayam vidyate kvachit. (1.25)

"One should concentrate one's mind on Om, for Om is Brahman beyond fear. For a man, ever fixed in Brahman, there can be no fear anywhere" (Mandukya Karika 1.25).

Pranavo hyaparam brahma pranavashcha parah smritah.
Apoorvo anantaro bahyo naparah pranavo vyayah. (1.26)

Sarvasya pranavo hyadiramadhyamantastathaiva cha.
Evam hi pranavam gyatva vyashnate tadanantram. (1.27)

Pranavam heeshram vidyatsarvasya hridi sansthitam.
Sarvavyapinamonkaram matva dhhero na shochati. (1.28)

Amaatro anantamatrashcha dwaitasyopashamah shivah.
Onkaro vidito yena sa munirnataro janah. (1.29)

"Om is surely the lower Brahman; and Om is considered to be the higher Brahman. Om is without cause, and without inside and outside; and it is undecaying. Om is indeed the beginning, middle, and end–everything. Having known this way indeed one attains immediately identity with the Self. One should know Om to be God seated in the hearts of all. Meditating on the all-pervasive Om, the intelligent man grieves no more. The Om, without measures and possessed of infinite dimension, is the auspicious entity where all duality ceases. He by whom Om is known, is the real sage, and not so is any other man" (Mandukya Karika 1:26-29).

3.2.7.13 OM in Satyartha Prakash

(Written by Maharishi Dayanand Saraswati, Founder of 'Arya Samaj' Movement)

Om shanno mitrah shun varunah shanno bhavatvarya ma.

Shanna indro brihaspatih shanno Vishnururukramah.
Namo btahmane Namaste vaayo tvamev pratyaksham brhmasi.
Tvamev pratyakshyam brahma vadishyami ritam vadishyami
Satyam vadishyami tanmamavatu tadvaktaaramavatu.
Avatu mama vatu vaktaaram.
Om shantishshantishshanti.

– (Satyarth Prakash Chapter 1 – Samullas 1)

We bow unto Thee (Brahma), O most Powerful Supreme Being. Thou alone art our Omniscient God whom we feel in the interior of our hearts. I will call Thee, Thee alone, my true God, Thy will, as truly revealed in the Vedas, will I obey and preach. I will be truthful in word, deed and thought. Thou art my shelter. Mayest thou protect me - Thy servant - who speaketh nought but truth, so that my understanding be firm in Thy Will, and never turn away from it. Thy Will is Truth and Righteousness. That which is contrary to it is Untruth and Unrighteousness. Mayest Thou again shelter and protect me. O Lord, be merciful and grant this, my prayer, for which I shall feel grateful unto Thee forever and ever. Peace! Peace!! Peace!!!

– (Satyarth Prakash Chapter 1 – Samullas 1)

3.3 Namah

As mentioned earlier, 'Namah' means to bow or to pay respect to.

3.4 Shivaya

As mentioned earlier, 'Shivaya' means to bow or to pay respect to Lord Shiva.

3.5 Om Namah Shivaya in Sarvalinga Stava

O Omkaresvara, Umamahesvara,
Ramesvara, Tryambakesvara,
Mahabalesvara, Mahakalesvara, Muktesvara,
Om Namah Sivaya.

O Jambukesvara, Kalahastisvara,
Tarakesvara, Paramesvara,
Narmadesvara, Nagesvara, Nanjundesvara,
Om Namah Sivaya.

O Ardhanarisvara, Kapalisvara,
Brihadisvara, Bhuvanesvara, Kumbhesvara,
Vriddhachalesvara, Ekambaresvara,
Om Namah Sivaya.

O Kailasapate, Pasupate,
Gauripate, Parvatipate,
Umapate, Sivakamipate,
Om Namah Sivaya.

O Visvesa, Tyagesa, Sarvesa,
Sundaresa, Mahesa, Jagadisa,
Ghusrunesa, Matribhutesa,
Om Namah Sivaya.

O Kailasanatha, Kashinatha,
Kedaranatha, Muktinatha,
Amaranatha, Pasupatinatha,
Om Namah Sivaya.

O Kasi Visvanatha, Kanchinatha,
Somanatha, Baijnatha, Vaidyanatha,
Tunganatha, Trilokinatha,
Om Namah Sivaya.

O Kalabhairava, Tripurantaka,
Nilalohita, Haro Hara,
Siva, Sambho, Sankara, Sadasiva,
Om Namah Sivaya.

O Mahadeva, Mahakala,
Nilakantha, Nataraja, Chandrasekhara,
Chidambaresa, Papavimochaka,
Om Namah Sivaya.

O Halasyasundara, Minakshisundara,
Kalyanasundara, Kadambavanasundara,
Srisaila-vasa, Virabhadra,
Om Namah Sivaya.

O Gauri Sankara, Gangadhara,
Dakshinamurte, Mrityunjaya,
Om Namo Bhagavate Rudraya,
Om Namah Sivaya.

O Vaikkatappa, Tiruvoniappa,
Chittambala, Ponnambala,
Chitsabhesa, Chidambaresa,
Om Namah Sivaya.

O Kamadahana, Brahmasiraschheda,
Kurma-Matsya-Varaha-Svarupa,
Virabhairava, Vrishabharudha,
Om Namah Sivaya.

O Kalantaka, Mallikarjuna,
Arunachala, Nandivahana,
Bhikshadana, Bhaktarakshaka,
Om Namah Sivaya.

O Bhimasankara, Bhasmadhara,
Pannagabhushana, Pinakadhari,
Trilochana, Trisulapane,
Om Namah Sivaya.

Who can describe Thy glory O Hara!
Even Sruti says Neti Neti,
Thou art Supreme Brahman,
Thou art full of auspicious qualities,
Om Namah Sivaya.

O Destroyer of Tripuras,
My silent adorations unto Thee,
Thou art Rudra, the destroyer,
Thou art bestower of Immortality,
Om Namah Sivaya.

Thy vehicle is the bull,
Tiger-skin is Thy garment,
Trident, Damaru, Axe, Are Thy instruments,
Om Namah Sivaya.

Snake is Thy ornament,
You are besmeared with ashes,
Ganga flows from Thy head,
Moon is Thy Chudamani,
Om Namah Sivaya.

You incarnated as Dakshinamurti,
To initiate Sanaka, Sanandana,
Into the mysteries of Brahma Jnana,
Through silence and Chinmudra,
Om Namah Sivaya.

Thy form speaks of renunciation,
Thou art embodiment of knowledge,
Thou art famous for Nritya,
Agada Bhum is Thy song,
Om Namah Sivaya.

You assumed the form of light,
Brahma and Vishnu failed
To measure Thee,
Thou art Infinity and Eternity,
Om Namah Sivaya.

You saved Markandeya, Manikkavasakar,
You blessed Kannappa, Tirunavukkarasu,
Tirujnanasambandhar, Sundarar,
Appar and Pattinathadiyar,
Om Namah Sivaya.

Thou art ocean of mercy,
Thou art giver of boons,
You blessed Arjuna and Bana,
You swallowed the poison,
And saved the world,
Om Namah Sivaya.

You destroyed the Cupid,
Thou art the Father
Of Ganesa and Subrahmanya,
You cut the head of proud Daksha,
Om Namah Sivaya.

Tripurasundari, Rajarajesvari,
Gauri, Chandi, Chamundi,
Durga, Annapurna,
Are Thy Saktis,
Om Namah Sivaya.

Thy garland is strung of skulls,
Thy matted lock is the abode for Ganga,
Thou dwellest in the cremation ground,
Thy form is terrible, Thou art Mahakala,
Thou art Death unto death itself,
Om Namah Sivaya.

Thou art the greatest Devotee of Hari,
Thou wearest in Thy head the Ganga,
Which flows from Hari's feet,
You initiate the Rama Taraka Mantra at Banaras,
Om Namah Sivaya.

Lord Rama worshipped Thee alone at Ramesvara,
You existed in sound as Sadasiva,
In the heart as Atma linga,
In the Vedas as Pranava,
Om Namah Sivaya.

O Hara! O Lord! O Siva!
Prostrations unto Thee again and again,
Let me remember Thee always,
Let me ever dwell in Thee,
Om Namah Sivaya.
Make me desireless, fearless and 'I' less,
Let me ever repeat Thy five letters,
Let me behold Thee everywhere,
Let me merge in Thee for ever,
Om Namah Sivaya.

He who sings or repeats or hears this 'Sarvalinga Stava' Morning and evening with faith, devotion and Bhava, Will be freed from all sins and diseases, Will attain son, wealth, prosperity.

3.6 Shiva Namaskaratha Mantra

Shiva Namaskaratha Mantra is one of the famous mantra used to get the blessing from God Shiva. It is very beautiful, audio of it is such that it recited in mind many times after listening.

It is a great mantra which glorifies Omnipresence, all knowledgeable Mahadev, Lord of death. This Mantra is also known as Lord Shiva's Most Powerful Mantra. Its beginning is by "Om Namo Hiranyabahave", means I bow to one who has golden hands.

Om Namo hiranyabahavey hiranyabaranaaya hiranyaroopaya
Ambika patayam uma pataye Pashupataye namo Namah

Yishanasarva vidhyana Yishwarasarva Bhootanaam
Brahmadipataye
Bramhnodipate Brahma Shivone Ashtusada Shivoom

Tatpurushaya vidmahe vagvishudhaaya dhimahe Tano Shiva
Prachodayate
Mahadevaaya Vidmahe Rudramoortaye Dhimahi Tanno Shiva
Prachodayate

Namaste Astu Bhagwan Vishweshwaraya Mahadevaaya
Trayambakaya Tripurantakaya Trikagni Kalaaya Kalagni
Rudraya Nilakanthay Mrityunjayaya Sarveshwaraya
Sadashivaya

Shriman Mahadevaaya Namaha
Shriman Mahadevaaya Namaha

This mantra is also for giving respect to Mahadeva, like Om Namah Shivaya or Rudrashtakam. In this mantra, several verses are from the Shiva Gayatri mantra. One name mentioned is Nilkanth which says how the throat of Mahadeva is blue. He takes poison from the sea to save the universe.

Another name is "Tripurantakaya" which indicates that Mahadeva wins over three cities created by Tripurasura.

3.7 Song of Lord Nataraja

Sivaya Nama Om Sivaya Namah,
Sivaya Nama Om Namah Sivaya,

O Lord Nataraja of Chidambaram,
King Dancer of Thillai Ambalam,
Beloved consort of Sivakami Sundari,
Bhuvanesvari, Rajarajesvari,
Destroyer of sin, bestower of prosperity,
Remover of suffering, giver of Immortality,

Sivaya Nama Om Sivaya Namah,
Sivaya Nama Om Namah Sivaya.

Holder of Trident, drinker of poison,
Master of Yogis, ruler in the Sun,
Dweller in Kailas, rider of Nandi
Destroyer of Cupid, Lord of Siddhi,
The three-eyed Lord, the five-faced God,
The blue-necked God, the God of gods,

Sivaya Nama Om Sivaya Namah,
Sivaya Nama Om Namah Sivaya.

Thou art my Guru and sole-refuge,
Salutations unto Thee O Lord of Mercy,
Bless me with Thy shower of Grace,
Let me behold Thy benign face,
Let me merge in Thee for ever,
This is my real fervent prayer.

Sivaya Nama Om Sivaya Namah,
Sivaya Nama Om Namah Sivaya.

Lord Siva gradually frees the individual souls from egoism, Karma and Maya. The Jivas gradually become disgusted with the sensual pleasures. They become balanced in pleasure and pain. Through the grace of the Lord they understand that Karma is the cause for births and deaths. They begin to do actions for the Lord, serve the devotees of the Lord and attain purity of mind. They understand that the soul or Siva is distinct from the body, senses and mind and is beyond the reach of mind and speech. They get initiation into the significance **of 'Om Namah Sivaya'**, the Panchakshara Mantra and meditate on Siva.

3.8 Shiva Mantras – 'Om Namah Shivaya Subham Subham Kuru Shivaya Namah Om'

3.8.1 Benefits of the Above Mantra

i. The above Mantra is highly auspicious. It generates the pleasure of Lord Shiva. It yields both worlds by enjoyment a salvation, confers cherished desires and brings about the happiness to the devotees of Shiva

ii. It is conducive to blessedness, fame, and longevity to those who seek heaven. Those who are free from desires derive the benefit of salvation.

iii. The devotee who repeats this mantra-in purity, hears or narrates this to any person, shall attain all desires.

iv. From the Adhara Sakti to the seat of the sacred love the devotee shall repeat the mantra. Om Shivaya Namah.

v. The japa of six syllables (Om Namah Shivaya) shall be performed always.

vi. Lord Shiva bad taught this great auspicious Mantra 'OM'. Omkara came out of HIS mouth. Originally it indicated him.

vii. Lord Shiva is the indicator and HE is the indicated. The mantra is identical with HIM. The repetition of this mantra is to verify his repeated remembrance.

viii. By the recitation of this root-mantra, the very enjoyment as well as salvation is achieved.

ix. The Mantra may be recited as directed by the Goddess (Parvati). This Om Mantra which is identical with Lord Shiva.

x. Your knowledge shall be stabilized. Permanent fortune shall stand by you. On the Chaturdashi day (4th Tithi) and on the day with Ardra Star (Ardra Nakshtra), the recitation of this Mantra will give you ever-lasting efficacy, name and fame.

xi. Remember that Lord Shiva creates the universe at the outset saying of "OM".

xii. The sages, the scholars, who realize and identify between the name and the sound know Lord Shiva as the single-syllabled OM.

xiii. Let the devotee practitioner, sitting in a retired place and restraining his senses, utter by inaudible repetition, the long pranava OM, in order to destroy all obstacles.

3. Repetition of Mantra (Japa) -

i. It is said that a Japa without the behest of the preceptor, holy rites, faith and the prescribe fees is fruitless though the behest might have been secured.

ii. If a Mantra is well practiced with the acquisition of behest, attended with holy rites, equipped with faith in Lord Shiva and accompanied by fee it is greatly efficacious, beneficial and fruitful.

iii. Dedicating yourself along with your possessions to the Lord and after uneventfully worshipping HIM to your capacity. You shall learn the Mantra and derive knowledge in due course of time.

iv. Lord Shiva recounts the procedure for acquiring the mantra. Without it the Mantra is futile and with it, it is efficacious.

   The futile ones are the following:

   a) Mantra acquired without permission.

   b) Devoid of holy rites.

   c) Devoid of faith.

   d) Devoid of full attention.

   e) That which has been prohibited.

   f) Permitted but devoid of gifts.

v. **The following Mantras are fruitful:**

   a) Achieved with permission.

   b) Attended with rituals.

c) Fully equipped with faith.

d) Where the mind fully dwells.

e) And attended with gifts (to the preceptor).

vi. The muttering of the Mantra with high, low or middle accentuation is called the verbal japa.

vii. The mumbling japa is the one where the tongue throbs and there is a sight utterance. It may not be heard by other or may be slightly heard.

viii. The mental japa is that where the series of letters are thought well and the words, their meaning are pondered over.

ix. The mumbling japa is hundred more times effications than verbal and the mental is a thousand times more effications than mumbling.

x. The japa shall be performed by means of the thumb in contact with other fingers (i.e. counting the japas on the rosary). If japa is performed without the thumb it is futile.

xi. All these are inimical to japa viz. anger, arrogance, inebriation and thirst, lethargy, spitting, yawning and seeing a dog or a base man.

xii. The native can perform japa while conversing with others.

xiii. Rosary for Mantras – If there are hundred and eight beads (of Rudraksha) that rosary is the most excellent (for japa).]

xiv. The benefit is infinite if the calculation (of Shiva's japa) is by knots of the Kusa grass or Rudraksha beads.

xv. Mantra Yoga – The practice and repetition of the japa along with meditation is Mantra-yoga.

xvi. If japa is performed in the house, it is ordinarily efficacious. In a holy forest or park, it is thousand times more. On the banks of a river, it is hundred times more.

xvii. The japa performed on the seashore in a divine pond, on a mountain, in a temple and in a sacred hermitage has a crore times the benefit. If it is in presence of Shiva (Linga) it is endless.

xviii. The japa with Rudra as the presiding deity is the most excellent, that with Vishnu as the presiding deity is the middling and that with Brahma as the presiding deity is of the lowest quality.

xix. One shall never perform Japa wearing a turban and a coat. If one is naked or one has loosened the knots of hair, or is dirty or is impure or has impure hands, he shall not perform Japa.

CHAPTER 4

About Lord Shiva

4.1 Introduction to Lord Shiva

Shiva means the auspicious one. Shiva is the reason why everything started.

Shiva is regarded as the destroyer, preserver and creator because he completes the Hindu cosmological cycle and ushers in the return of creation. He wears a chignon with curls and has a vertical third eye in the middle of his forehead. He often is depicted with four arms, carrying a string of beads, a symbol of his teaching, and a trident. The beads are called Rudraksha beads, a reference to his early name.

Lord Shiva is the magnificent, supreme divinity in the oldest civilization. He is incomparable, the complete Lord in all aspect who exist in a dual phase. The first phase is formless in which he doesn't have any reality, whereas, the second form is the most charismatic and entrancing. Shiva is the Lord of consciousness, infinite strength, graciousness, knowledge, compassion, Creation, and destruction. Everything depends on him. He is the supreme ruler of the multiverse, beyond the level of human perception.

He manifested himself in physical form as Rudra so that world could have an idea of his representation. He is the ultimate light, emerged himself on his will. He is infinite voidness whose Shakti (energy) is within everyone. You cannot understand Shiva without understanding yourself. He is already within you, and you are within him. It is the same thing. You need to discover him inside in the form of your inner peace. Shiva doesn't want anything from us; He already has everything within him. He is the last giver who only knows to give. He never asked anything in return of anything which he gave to us. The innocence of Shiva is cherished the most by Shiva devotees all over the world. Shiva is kind who gets happy with just offering of a Bilva leaf. Everything about Lord Shiva is attractive. Hence, there are limitless devotees of Shiva who admire every virtue of Shiva's physical state; learning more about Shiva will open nectar of blissfulness for you.

Shiva is worshipped as the ascetic god, remote when in meditation but also at times wild, passionate, and loving. As Lord of the Dance, he both destroys and creates the universe. His cosmic dance visualizes the cycles of creation and destruction in human lives, in the history of nations, and in the universe. Shiva is also manifest in a phallic emblem called a linga, and it is in this form that he is most often portrayed in the inner sanctum of his temples. Worshippers of Shiva believe that he is the supreme god who contains and controls all creation.

The name of Shiva does not appear in the Vedas, but he was earlier known as Rudra, or the Fearful and Destructive One. Through the power of destruction, which in the most intensified form makes him a Bhairava ('The Terrible Destroyer'), remains Shiva's principal attribute, the corollary of that attribute, namely creation or fertility, is also central to the identity of Shiva. This aspect of Shiva is represented by the lingam, or phallus, which is worshipped as a representation of Shiva. Sometimes the female genitals, or yoni, are also placed alongside the lingam. These are not the only iconic representations of Shiva: he appears as the yogi, having all the powers acquired by meditation, penance, and a life of austerity, or as the naked ascetic Digambara, with matted hair and a body smeared with ashes. To begin to enumerate Shiva's various forms, epithets, and representations is to unravel the multiple layering of Indian civilization.

In the Vedic verses Shiva was known as Rudra, a minor deity that protected cattle and was associated with the howl of the wind and healing herbs. He had both and positive and negative side: he could bring disease and he could cure it. In the Rig Veda he is mentioned only three times. Over time Rudra absorbed merged with an early fertility god and became Shiva. By the second century B.C. Shiva had become popular as indicated by the large number stone lingams, symbols of Shiva, found in archaeological sites. In the A.D. 2nd century there were Shiva cults made up of devotees who made lewd gestures at women and sneering noises during ceremonies and slept in the ashes left behind from funeral pyres. By the seventh century Shiva had become a more mainstream Hindu God.

4.2 Shiva Lives on Mt. Meru (Mt. Kailas in Tibet)

The god Shiva is the other great figure in the modern pantheon. In contrast to the regal attributes of Vishnu, Shiva is a figure of renunciation. A favourite image portrays him as an ascetic, performing meditation alone in the fastness of the Himalayas.

There he sits on a tiger skin, clad only in a loincloth, covered with sacred ash that gives his skin a gray color. His trident is stuck into the ground next to him. Around his neck is a snake. From his matted hair, tied in a topknot, the river Ganga (Ganges) descends to the earth. His neck is blue, a reminder of the time he drank the poison that emerged while gods and demons competed to churn the milk ocean. But behind this image is the cosmic lord who, through the very power of his meditating consciousness, expands the entire universe and all beings in it. Although he appears to be hard to attain, in reality Shiva is a loving deity who saves those devotees who are wholeheartedly dedicated to him.

4.3 Shiva as Nataraj

Natraj dancing form of Lord Shiva is one of the renowned art forms of Shiva. It is artistic and can be found anywhere in the world. Shiva's dancing form is known as the dance of creation and destruction. The dancing form of Shiva clarifies that if you don't contemplate; you will never liberate from the cycle of Maya. The Dancing form of Shiva is compatible with modern scientific ideas. It has the element of art, physiology, psychologically, spirituality, and cosmology. Lord Shiva in the dancing mudra is exceptional in various aspects. On closely following the Shiva's dancing form, we start realizing who we are, and from where we have come?

Hindus believe his powers of destruction and recreation are used even now to destroy the illusions and imperfections of this world, paving the way for beneficial change. According to Hindu belief, this destruction is not arbitrary, but constructive. Shiva is therefore seen as the source of both good and evil and is regarded as the one who combines many contradictory elements.

Natraj Dancing is the metaphor of the cosmic dance; it should not be seen only from the religious aspect. It is a beautiful example of art, science, and religion. Modern science doesn't have something like Dancing Shiva, which is spiritual by origin but scientific in its fundamental aspect.

To understand it clearly, Let us dig into it. 1 There is a large circle behind dancing Natraj. It represents the time, matter, space, and energy managed by Shiva. 2 - Fire flames are coming out of the round; it comes out on Shiva's insistence. It is the process of making a vacuum in the voidness so that process of universe formation or creation could get started. It also represents the Kala-chakra only Shiva has the key to start, hold, reverse, and stop the Kaal-Chakra.

Shiva typically carries a **trident** and has a **third** eye in his forehead, signifying his all-seeing nature. He often has a serpent wrapped around him like a scarf and wears a skull and the crescent moon in his matted hair piled high upon his head. While other gods are depicted in lavish surroundings, Shiva is dressed in simple animal skin and in austere settings, usually in a yogic position. Parvati, whenever she is present, is always at the side of Shiva. Their relationship is one of equality.

Shiva is represented with the following features:

i. **Third eye:** The extra eye represents the wisdom and insight that Shiva has. It is also believed to be the source of his untamed energy. On one occasion, when Shiva was distracted in the midst of worship by the love god, Kama, Shiva opened his third eye in anger.

Kama was consumed by the fire that poured forth, and only returned to life when Parvati intervened.

ii. **Cobra necklace**: This signifies Shiva's power over the most dangerous creatures in the world. Some traditions also say that the snake represents Shiva's power of destruction and recreation. The snake sheds its skin to make way for new, smooth skin.

iii. **Vibhuti** is three lines drawn horizontally across the forehead in white ash. They represent Shiva's all-pervading nature, his superhuman power and wealth. Also, they cover up his powerful third eye. Members of Shaivism often draw vibhuti lines across their forehead.

iv. **The Trident:** The three-pronged trident represents the three functions of the Hindu triumvirate.

Shiva is sometimes represented as half man, half woman. His figure is split half way down the body, one half showing his body and the second half that of Parvati's. Shiva is also represented by Shiva linga. This is a phallic statue, representing the raw power of Shiva and his masculinity. Hindus believe it represents the seed of the universe, demonstrating Shiva's quality of creation. Worshipers of Shiva celebrate Mahashivaratri, a festival at which the Shiva linga is bathed in water, milk and honey and worshiped.

v. **Lingams (or lingas)** are the phallic symbols that honour Shiva and represent male energy, rebirth, fertility and the creative forces of the universe. They are found in varying sizes in many Hindu temples. A typical one is shaped like an erect phallus and made

> of polished stone. The vertical shaft is sometimes divided into the parts symbolizing the Hindu Trinity, with the upper rounded part associated with Shiva, the middle part linked to Vishnu, and the bottom part representing Brahma. According to the *Shiva Purana* "it is not the *linga* that is worshiped but the one whose symbol it is.

Lingams are usually set on a round base called a *yoni,* which represents Shakti and the female force. A channel is carved on the base to allow ablutions to flow out. Shiva worshipers like to pour cow's milk on lingams, sprinkle them with flowers and red powder and make offering of fruits and sweets. The lingam and the base together are a sort of ying and yang statue that symbolizes the entire universe and the union and interaction between male and female power.

The trident is another symbol associated with Shiva. The three forks are said to represent creation, preservation and destruction. Depictions of Shiva with three faces also represent the same balanced trilogy: two of the faces are usually opposites: maker and destroyer, or acetic and family-man, with the third face in the middle being a peaceful, reconciling force.

Shiva is closely associated with Varanasi and death. It is said that anyone who dies in Varanasi will join Shiva straight away in Mt. Meru regardless of how much bad karma they have accumulated. Shiva is also closely associated with the Ganges, and India›s other holy river.

Devi›s best-known incarnation is Parvati, Shiva›s primary and eternal wife. Shiva and Parvati are held up as the perfect example of marital bliss by many Hindus, and one is rarely depicted without the other. Hindus believe Shiva and Parvati live in the Kailash Mountains in the Himalayas. Parvati is the daughter of the sacred Himalayas. Renowned for her gentleness, she is regarded as the most benign and conservative of Shiva›s partners. She and Shiva have two sons: Skanda, the god of War, and Ganesh the popular elephant-headed god.

Nataraj, an incarnation of Shiva, is the goddess of dance. It is often depicted in old bronze statues with four arms and one leg raised and the other crushing Apasmara, a dwarf-demon associated with confusion and ignorance. One hand assumes the gesture of protection, one points to a raised foot, one hold the drum that keeps the beat of the rhythm of creation and the fourth holds the fire of dissolution.

Nandi, the sacred bull, is Shiva's mount when he rides through the heavens. It represents fertility; is often as white as the Himalayan peaks; and marks the entrance to Shiva temples. A crescent moon encircling Shiva's third eye is a symbol of the Nandi bull. Two other deities are considered their children. Elephant-headed Ganesha is the god who removes obstacles and is worshipped at the start of any undertaking; his vehicle is the mouse. Skanda, a warlike youth, rides the peacock.

Shiva and Parvati have two sons, who have entire cycles of myths and legends and bhakti cults in their own right. One son is called variously Kartikeya (identified with the planet Mars) or Skanda (the god of war or Subrahmanya). He is extremely handsome, carries a spear, and rides a peacock. According to some traditions, he emerged motherless from Shiva when the gods needed a great warrior to conquer an indestructible demon.

Another son of Shiva and Parvati is Ganesh, or Ganapati, the Lord of the Ganas (the hosts of Shiva), who has a male human's body with four arms and the head of an elephant. One myth claims that he originated directly from Parvati's body and entered into a quarrel with Shiva, who cut off his human head and replaced it later with the head of the first animal he found, which happened to be an elephant. For most worshipers, Ganesh is the first deity invoked during any ceremony because he is the god of wisdom and remover of obstacles.

4.4 Rudra

Shiva as we know him today shares many features with the Vedic god Rudra, and both Shiva and Rudra are viewed as the same personality in Hindu scriptures. The two names are used synonymously. Rudra, a Rigvedic deity with fearsome powers, was the god of the roaring storm. He is usually portrayed in accordance with the element he represents as a fierce, destructive deity. In Rig Veda 2.33, he is described as the "Father of the Rudras", a group of storm gods. Rudra is an ambiguous god, peripheral in the Vedic pantheon, possibly indicating non-Vedic origins.

During the development of the Hindu synthesis attributes of the Buddha were transferred by Brahmins to Shiva, who was also linked with Rudra. The Rigveda has 3 out of 1,028 hymns dedicated to Rudra, and he finds occasional mention in other hymns of the same text. Hymn 10.92 of the Rigveda states that deity Rudra has two natures, one wild and cruel (Rudra), another that is kind and tranquil (Shiva).

The term Shiva also appears simply as an epithet, that means "kind, auspicious", one of the adjectives used to describe many different Vedic deities. While fierce ruthless natural phenomenon and storm-related Rudra is feared in the hymns of the Rigveda, the beneficial rains he brings are welcomed as Shiva aspect of him. This healing, nurturing, life-enabling aspect emerges in the Vedas as Rudra-Shiva, and in post-Vedic literature ultimately as Shiva who combines the destructive and constructive powers, the terrific and the gentle, as the ultimate recycler and rejuvenator of all existence.

4.5 Agni

Rudra and Agni have a close relationship. The identification between Agni and Rudra in the Vedic literature was an important factor in the process of Rudra's gradual transformation into Rudra-Shiva. The identification of Agni with Rudra is explicitly noted in the Nirukta, an important early text on etymology, which says, "Agni is also called Rudra."

In the Śatarudrīya, some epithets of Rudra, such as Sasipañjara ("Of golden red hue as of flame") and Tivaṣīmati ("Flaming bright"), suggest a fusing of the two deities. Agni is said to be a bull, and Lord Shiva possesses a bull as his vehicle, Nandi. The horns of Agni, who is sometimes characterized as a bull, are mentioned. In medieval sculpture, both Agni and the form of Shiva known as Bhairava have flaming hair as a special feature.

4.6 Indra

The Saivite fertility myths and some of the phallic characteristics of Shiva are inherited from Indra. Both are associated with mountains, rivers, male fertility, fierceness, fearlessness, warfare, the transgression of established mores, the Aum sound, the Supreme Self. In the Rig Veda the term śiva is used to refer to Indra. (2.20.3, Indra, like Shiva, is likened to a bull. In the Rig Veda, Rudra is the father of the Maruts, but he is never associated with their warlike exploits as is Indra.

4.7 Shiva-Related Literature

He who sees himself in all beings,
And all beings in him,
attains the highest Brahman,
not by any other means.

– Kaivalya Upanishad

Shaiva devotees and ascetics are mentioned in Patanjali's Mahābhāṣya (2nd-century BCE) and in the Mahabharata.

Shaiva Upanishads are a group of 14 minor Upanishads of Hinduism variously dated from the last centuries of the 1st millennium BCE through the 17th century. These extol Shiva as the metaphysical unchanging reality Brahman and the Atman (Self),[and include sections about rites and symbolisms related to Shiva.

The Shaiva Puranas, particularly the Shiva Purana and the Linga Purana, present the various aspects of Shiva, mythologies, cosmology and pilgrimage (Tirtha) associated with him. The Shiva-related Tantra literature, composed between the 8th and 11th centuries, are regarded in devotional dualistic Shaivism as Sruti. Dualistic Shaiva Agamas which consider Self within each living being and Shiva as two separate realities (dualism, dvaita), are the foundational texts for Shaiva Siddhanta. Other Shaiva Agamas teach that these are one reality (monism, advaita), and that Shiva is the Self, the perfection and truth within each living being. In Shiva related sub-traditions, there are ten dualistic Agama texts, eighteen qualified monism-cum-dualism Agama texts and sixty-four monism Agama texts.

Shiva-related literature developed extensively across India in the 1st millennium CE and through the 13th century, particularly in Kashmir and Tamil Shaiva traditions. The monist Shiva literature posit absolute oneness, that is Shiva is within every man and woman, Shiva is within every living being, Shiva is present everywhere in the world including all non-living being, and there is no spiritual difference between life, matter, man and Shiva. The various dualistic and monist Shiva-related ideas were welcomed in medieval southeast Asia, inspiring numerous Shiva-related temples, artwork and texts in Indonesia, Myanmar, Cambodia, Laos, Vietnam, Thailand and Malaysia, with syncretic integration of local pre-existing theologies.

4.8 Shiva, The Auspicious One

Shiva ('The Auspicious One'), also known as Mahadeva 'The Great God' is one of the principal deities of Hinduism. He is the Supreme Being in Shaivism, one of the major traditions within Hinduism.

Shiva has pre-Vedic tribal roots, and the figure of Shiva as we know him today is an amalgamation of various older non-Vedic and Vedic deities, including the Rigvedic storm god Rudra who may also have non-Vedic origins, into a single major deity.

Shiva is known as "The Destroyer" within the Trimurti, the triple deity of supreme divinity that includes Brahma and Vishnu. In the Shaivite tradition, Shiva is the Supreme Lord who creates, protects and transforms the universe. In the Shakta tradition, the Goddess, or Devi, is described as one of the supreme, yet Shiva is revered along with Vishnu and Brahma. A goddess is stated to be the energy and creative power (Shakti) of each, with Parvati (Sati) the equal complementary partner of Shiva. He is one of the five equivalent deities in Panchayatana puja of the Smarta tradition of Hinduism.

Shiva is the primal Atman (Self) of the universe. There are many both benevolent and fearsome depictions of Shiva. In benevolent aspects, he is depicted as an omniscient Yogi who lives an ascetic life on Mount Kailash as well as a householder with wife Parvati and his two children, Ganesha and Kartikeya. In his fierce aspects, he is often depicted slaying demons. Shiva is also known as Adiyogi Shiva, regarded as the patron god of yoga, meditation and arts.

The iconographical attributes of Shiva are the serpent around his neck, the adorning crescent moon, the holy river Ganga flowing from his matted hair, the third eye on his forehead, the trishula or trident, as his weapon, and the damaru drum. He is usually worshipped in the aniconic form of lingam. Shiva is a pan-Hindu deity, revered widely by Hindus, in India, Nepal, Sri Lanka and Indonesia (especially in Java and Bali).

The Sanskrit word "śiva" (also transliterated as shiva) means, means "auspicious, propitious, gracious, benign, kind, benevolent, friendly". The roots of śiva in folk etymology are śī which means "in whom all things lie, pervasiveness" and va which means "embodiment of grace".

The word Shiva is used as an adjective in the Rig Veda (approximately 1700–1100 BC), as an epithet for several Rigvedic deities, including Rudra. The term Shiva also connotes "liberation, final emancipation" and "the auspicious one", this adjective sense of usage is addressed to many deities in Vedic layers of literature. The term evolved from the Vedic Rudra-Shiva to the noun Shiva in the Epics and the Puranas, as an auspicious deity who is the "creator, reproducer and dissolver".

The Vishnu sahasranama interprets Shiva to have multiple meanings: "The Pure One", and "the One who is not affected by three Guṇas of Prakṛti (Sattva, Rajas, and Tamas)".

Shiva is known by many names such as Viswanatha (lord of the universe), Mahadeva, Mahandeo, Mahasu, Mahesha, Maheshvara, Shankara, Shambhu, Rudra, Hara, Trilochana, Devendra (chief of the gods), Neelakanta, Subhankara, Trilokinatha (lord of the three realms), and Ghrneshwar (lord of compassion). The highest reverence for Shiva in Shaivism is reflected in his epithets Mahādeva ("Great god"; mahā "Great" and deva "god"), Maheśvara ("Great Lord"; mahā "great" and īśvara "lord"), and Parameśvara ("Supreme Lord").

Sahasranama are medieval Indian texts that list a thousand names derived from aspects and epithets of a deity. There are at least eight different versions of the Shiva Sahasranama, devotional hymns (stotras) listing many names of Shiva. The version appearing in Book 13 (Anuśāsanaparvan) of the Mahabharata provides one such list. Shiva also has Dasha-Sahasranamas (10,000 names) that are found in the Mahanyasa. The Shri Rudram Chamakam, also known as the Śatarudriya, is a devotional hymn to Shiva hailing him by many names.

4.9 Assimilation of Traditions

The Shiva-related tradition is a major part of Hinduism, found all over the Indian subcontinent, such as India, Nepal, Sri

Lanka, and Southeast Asia, such as Bali, Indonesia. Shiva has pre-Vedic tribal roots, having "his origins in primitive tribes, signs and symbols." The figure of Shiva as we know him today is an amalgamation of various older deities into a single figure, due to the process of Sanskritization and the emergence of the Hindu synthesis in post-Vedic times. How the persona of Shiva converged as a composite deity is not well documented, a challenge to trace and has attracted much speculation.

An example of assimilation took place in Maharashtra, where a regional deity named Khandoba is a patron deity of farming and herding castes. The foremost centre of worship of Khandoba in Maharashtra is in Jejuri. Khandoba has been assimilated as a form of Shiva himself, in which case he is worshipped in the form of a lingam. Khandoba's varied associations also include an identification with Surya and Karttikeya.

4.10 Pre-Historic Art

Fifteen-thousand years ago, when Adiyogi first began the transmission of the yogic sciences to his seven disciples—the Saptarishis—he began expounding many incredible things about the entire mechanics of human existence. Scholars have interpreted early prehistoric paintings at the Bhimbetka rock shelters, considered to be from pre-10,000 BCE period, as Shiva dancing, Shiva's trident, and his mount Nandi. Rock paintings from Bhimbetka, depicting a figure with a trident or trishula, have been described as Nataraja which dates to the mesolithic.

4.11 Indus Valley and the Pashupati Seal

Of several Indus valley seals that show animals, one seal that has attracted attention shows a large central figure, either horned or wearing a horned headdress and possibly ithyphallic, seated in a posture reminiscent of the Lotus position, surrounded by animals. This figure was named by early excavators of Mohenjo-daro as Pashupati (Lord of Animals, Sanskrit paśupati), an epithet of the later Hindu deities Shiva and Rudra.

4.12 Who is Shiva?

When we say "Shiva," there are two fundamental aspects that we are referring to. The word "Shiva" literally means "that which is not." Today, modern science is proving to us that everything comes from nothing and goes back to nothing. The basis of existence and the fundamental quality of the cosmos is vast nothingness. The galaxies are just a small happening – a sprinkling. The rest is all vast empty space, which is referred to as Shiva. That is the womb from which everything is born, and that is the oblivion into which everything is sucked back. Everything comes from Shiva and goes back to Shiva.

Shiva is that nothingness, the dark empty void of space, from which all creation - the stars, planets, galaxies, mountains, oceans, all living beings, etc. - manifest and into which all creations disintegrate. Shiva is not a person but is a principle.; It is a concept. It is called the Shiva Tattva, which is an all-pervading consciousness that fills up this nothingness.

Today, even astronomy tells us that 99.99% of the universe is just empty - nothingness. So, 95% of this is 'dark matter' and 'dark energy', so-called because they do not reflect, absorb or emit light and hence cannot be seen - ever.

Shiva means that which is innocent, benevolent, beautiful, transcendental, and absolute. There is a certain correlation between the five elements, seven layers of our being, and our consciousness. Shiva energy permeates through the universe and you will find that it is possible to experience the Shiva Tattva - absolute nothingness - within us.

So Shiva is described as a non-being, not as a being. Shiva is not described as light, but as darkness. Humanity has gone about eulogizing light only because of the nature of the visual apparatus that they carry. Otherwise, the only thing that is always, is darkness. Light is a limited happening in the sense that any source of light – whether a light bulb or the sun – will eventually lose its ability to give out light. Light is not eternal. It is always a limited possibility because it happens and it ends. Darkness is a much bigger possibility than light. Nothing needs to burn, it is always – it is eternal. Darkness is everywhere. It is the only thing that is all pervading. We have known this concept of Shiva for thousands of years.

On another level, when we say "Shiva," we are referring to a certain yogi, the Adiyogi or the first yogi, and also the Adi Guru, the first Guru, who is the basis of what we know as the yogic science today. Yoga does not mean standing on your head or holding your breath. Yoga is the

science and technology to know the essential nature of how this life is created and how it can be taken to its ultimate possibility.

So "Shiva" refers to both "that which is not," and Adiyogi because in many ways, they are synonymous. This being, who is a yogi, and that non-being, which is the basis of the existence, are the same, because to call someone a yogi means he has experienced the existence as himself. If you have to contain the existence within you even for a moment as an experience, you have to be that nothingness. Only nothingness can hold everything. Something can never hold everything. A vessel cannot hold an ocean. This planet can hold an ocean, but it cannot hold the solar system. The solar system can hold these few planets and the sun, but it cannot hold the rest of the galaxy. If you go progressively like this, ultimately you will see it is only nothingness that can hold everything. The word "yoga" means "union." A yogi is one who has experienced the union. That means, at least for one moment, he has been absolute nothingness.

When we talk about Shiva as "that which is not," and Shiva as a yogi, in a way they are synonymous, yet they are two different aspects. Because India is a dialectical culture, we shift from this to that and that to this effortlessly. One moment we talk about Shiva as the ultimate, the next moment we talk about Shiva as the man who gave us this whole process of yoga.

The word "yoga" means "union." A yogi is one who has experienced the union. That means, at least for one moment, he has been absolute nothingness. When we talk about Shiva as "that which is not," and Shiva as a yogi, in a way they are synonymous, yet they are two different aspects. One moment we talk about Shiva as the ultimate, the next moment we talk about Shiva as the man who gave us this whole process of yoga.

In the yogic culture, Shiva is not seen as a God. He was a being who walked this land and lived in the Himalayan region. As the very source of the yogic traditions, his contribution in the making of human consciousness is too phenomenal to be ignored. This predates all religion. Before people devised divisive ways of fracturing humanity to a point where it seems almost impossible to fix, the most powerful tools necessary to raise human consciousness were realized and propagated. Every possible way in which you could approach and transform the human mechanism into an ultimate possibility was explored thousands of years ago.

4.13 Lord Shiva and His Nineteen Avatars

Hailed as Bholenath, Mahadev, Shankar and various other names, Lord Shiva has incarnated several times to serve multiple purposes.

Lord Shiva is one of the towering deities of the Hindu trinity. He is hailed as the "destroyer" while Brahma is the "creator" and Vishnu is the "protector". Nonetheless, the "destruction" referred to here is not the dogmatic destruction of creation but the intrinsic negative human traits, imperfections and illusions. And this "destruction" paves the way for creation all over again. Therefore, Lord Shiva could be best described as a "constructive destroyer."

This Hindu deity, in a human form, is seen sitting in a meditative posture. It is Lord Shiva who is also worshipped in the form of a Linga. It is said that the Linga form of Lord Shiva came into being on the Chaturdashi Tithi, Krishna Paksha in Phalguna month (as per the Purnimant calendar).

This auspicious day is also believed to be when Lord Shiva (Purusha) united with Parvati (Shakti). Therefore, the day, popular as Maha Shivaratri, commemorates the Lord and his consort's marriage. Hailed as Bholenath, Mahadev, Shankar and various other names, Lord Shiva has incarnated several times to serve multiple purposes. Ahead of Maha Shivratri this year, learn more about the avatars of Lord Shiva.

Following are the nineteen avatars of Lord Shiva:

(i) Piplaad Avatar

This avatar of Lord Shiva was born to Sage Dadhichi and his wife, Swarcha. However, he lost his parent's son after his birth. He was raised by his aunt Dadhimati. As he grew up and learnt about the cause of his father's death, Piplaad cursed Shani Dev (Saturn). He wanted to avenge Shani Dev for causing troubling his father during his lifetime. As a result, Shani Dev fell from the galaxy. However, after the Devas intervened, Piplaad agreed to forgive Shani by saying that none below sixteen would get affected by his adverse effects. Therefore, those who have Shani Dosha worship Lord Shiva.

(ii) Nandi Avatar

This form of Lord Shiva was born to Sage Shilada. The sage performed intense penance to seek Lord Shiva's blessings and asked for a child who would remain immortal. Therefore, pleased by Sage's devotion, Lord Shiva took birth as Nandi, who then became the gate-keeper of Kailasha (Lord Shiva's heavenly abode) and the mount of the Lord.

(iii) Veerabhadra Avatar

The Veerabhadra avatar of Lord Shiva is one of his fiercest forms. Lord Shiva incarnated as Veerabhadra after his wife Sati's death. The Veerabhadra form of Lord Shiva destroyed King Daksha's Yagya and beheaded him for being responsible for Sati's death.

(iv) Bhairava Avatar

The Bhairava Avatar also is one of the fiercest avatars of Lord Shiva. Referred to as Dandapani, the Bhairava Avatar punishes those who are greedy, lustful and arrogant. These negative traits often lead to one's downfall, and hence the purpose of the Bhairava avatar.

(v) Ashwatthama Avatar

Guru Dronacharya had performed intense penance to please Lord Shiva. He wanted the Lord to be born as his son. Therefore, pleased by Guru Dronacharya's devotion, Lord Shiva took birth as Ashwatthama, an able warrior who played a pivotal role in the Mahabharata.

(vi) Sharabha Avatar

This form of Lord Shiva appeared to calm Lord Narasimha after the latter killed demon Hiranyakashipu. The Sharabha avatar is one of its kind. The Lord appeared as a being that partly looked like a lion and bird. In some texts, the Sharabha avatar is said to have eight legs.

(vii) Grihapati Avatar

The Grihapati avatar of Lord Shiva was born to a sage named Vishwanar and his wife, who lived on the Narmada banks. The sage's consort wanted Lord Shiva to be born as her son. Therefore, the sage performed intense penance in Kashi. A few days later, pleased by Vishwanar's devotion, Lord Shiva was born as Grihapati to the sage and his wife.

(viii) Durvasa Avatar

This avatar of Lord Shiva was born to Sage Atri and his wife, Anusuya. He was known for being short-tempered and commanded respect both from the humans as well as the Devas.

(ix) Rishabha Avatar

As per a legend associated with this avatar, Lord Shiva appeared as a bull to kill the sons born to Lord Vishnu and the Patala Loka women. Lord Vishnu's sons caused destruction, and hence at Lord Brahma's behest, Lord Shiva appeared as Rishabha to save creation.

(x) Yatinath Avatar

The Yatinath avatar of Lord Shiva appeared to test a tribal couple, who were known for their hospitality. The tribal man named Aahuk lost his life while safeguarding his guest, Yatinath. Instead of mourning, his wife took pride in him for giving away his life for the sake of a guest. Pleased by the couple's devotion, Lord Shiva blessed them by saying that they would be born as Nala and Damayanti in their next birth.

(xi) Hanuman

Lord Hanuman is said to be the eleventh avatar of Lord Shiva. He was born to Mata Anjani and Kesari.

(xii) Krishna Darshan Avatar

This avatar of Lord Shiva appeared to emphasize the importance of Yagya and the importance of remaining detached. This legend is associated with a king named Nabhag, his father Shradhadeva and Sage Angiras.

(xiii) Bhikshuvarya Avatar

As the name suggests, Lord Shiva appeared as a beggar to save the child of a King named Sathyaratha. Since the child had lost his parents, he was brought up by a poor woman with Lord Shiva's blessings.

(xiv) Sureshwar Avatar

This avatar of Lord Shiva appeared in Indra Dev's disguise to test the devotion of a young boy named Upamanyu. The young boy passed the litmus test and succeeded in making Lord Shiva reveal himself.

(xv) Keerat Avatar

This avatar of Lord Shiva appeared to test the bravery of Arjuna. When the Pandavas were in exile, Arjuna meditated to seek Lord Shiva's Pashupata. As he was meditating, a demon named Mooka transformed into a boar to kill Arjuna. Lord Shiva's Keerat Avatar and Arjuna both killed the boar with their respective arrows. Initially, Arjun couldn't recognize Lord Shiva, but eventually, he realized that only the Lord could be a better archer than him.

(xvi) Sunatnartak Avatar

The Sunatnartak avatar of Lord Shiva appeared in the Himalayan King's court and danced with his damru. In the end, he put forward a marriage proposal and expressed his desire to marry Parvati.

(xvii) Brahmachari Avatar

When Sati took birth as Parvati and performed intense penance to please Lord Shiva, the latter appeared before her as a Brahmachari. He hurled abuses at Shiva to test Parvati's devotion. And Parvati, who loved Lord Shiva more than anyone else, gave a fitting reply to the Brahmachari. Eventually, Lord Shiva revealed himself and blessed Parvati.

(xviii) Yaksheshwar Avatar

The Yaksheshwar avatar of Lord Shiva appeared to crush the pride/complacency of the Devas after they consumed Amrit, the divine nectar. He asked them to cut a blade of grass, and they failed to destroy it even with their combined powers. Subsequently, they apologized to Lord Shiva.

(xix) Avadhut Avatar

Lord Shiva appeared as Avadhoot to crush the ego of Indra Dev.

4.14 Some Aspects and Manifestations of Lord Shiva

The Saiva tradition identifies Lord Siva or Shiva as the formless, eternal, mysterious, and supreme being having many aspects, potencies, and dimensions. He is considered both transcendental and immanent, who cannot be quantified and qualified objectively with our limited awareness. He is beyond our mind and senses, but within the reach of our experience and awakening. Various schools of Shaivism and the scriptures that form their basis allude to some important aspects of Shiva, as experienced by the awakened jivas in their transcendental states, which are mentioned below.

(i) Shiva as Nirguna Brahman

At the highest level, lord Siva is Sadashiva, Parameswara, or Paramashiva. In his formless (nirguna) aspect, he is the transcendental formless reality, the highest and the most unknown, who is Brahman Himself without qualities and attributes, the supreme lord, the eternal truth, the absolute, infinite, timeless, indivisible, entirely subjective Truth, which is beyond the senses and mind, without time. He is the end of all spiritual practices, the experience of pure consciousness and bliss in the state of samadhi or union. by experiencing which everything is known and realized. He is the eternal mystery mentioned in the Kena Upanishad, whom Uma Haimavati refers as the "Spirit Supreme", by knowing whom Indra excelled all other devas and became the ruler of the heavens. According to Shiva purana even Brahma and Vishnu attained the level of Trinity because of their past devotion to Nirguna Siva.

(ii) Shiva as Saguna Brahman

As the awakened supreme self, Shiva is Maheshwara or Mahashiva, the Lord of the manifest universe. As the awakened supreme self, he is saguna Brahman, the cosmic lord, who combines within himself the roles of creation, maintenance, destruction, concealment and liberation. He performs these five functions through his five supreme energies: pure consciousness (chit-shakti, bliss (ananda-shakti), will power (icchha-shakti), pure knowledge (jnana-shakti) and dynamic power (kriya-shakti).

As manifest Brahman, he projects the material and objective universe through his dynamic power (shakti) and projects into himself, like a reflection in a mirror, all that he creates. The creation is but his conscious dream, an alternate reality that cannot be entirely categorized as false or illusory. He is the Purusha of the Vedas, the cosmic male, who creates Prakriti, the cosmic female and then establishes himself in it in order to manifest the objective reality in which he conceals himself from himself exists as deluded jivas. He Himself creates, Himself preservs, Himself destroys, Himself obscures and then grants himself mukti, Himself, the all- pervading lord. He is also the source of all knowledge, the Agamas and the Tantras come from him.

(iii) Shiva as the Lord of a Functional Universe

At the next lower level he is Ishwara or Shiva or Rudra, representing a functional aspect of Mahashiva, performing the role of a destroyer. In this role, he is responsible for the regeneration and renewal of the material and objective universe and its various components through destruction and degeneration. In this functional aspect he facilitates the illusory movement of kala (time) from one phase (yuga) to another. He is Hara and Shankara, the lord with a thousand names, who is seated on the mountains of Kailash, with Parvati and his whole entourage of devas, gods, siddhas, shiva ganas, myriad yogis and devotees enjoying his darshan (vision). In this role he facilitates the spiritual progress of humanity. He evolves the subtle beings into gross and then the gross beings into subtle. Through his grace (anugraha), he destroys our karma, impurities and bonds and facilitates our spiritual evolution. He makes possible the flow of divine consciousness into our earth consciousness using himself as the conduit and brings forth all the tantras and agamas.

(iv) Shiva as Jiva, the Embodied and Deluded Soul

The jivas are the deluded aspect of Shiva. According to some schools of Shaivism, they are not created by any one and exist just like Shiva eternally. Their number also remains constant which means they retain their individuality even after attaining liberation from the bonds of objectivity. According to other schools, jivas and Shiva represent the same reality. There is actually no difference between the two or at the most the relationship is that of difference and non-difference (bhedaabheda). The deluded being are subject to the impurities of anava (finiteness), delusion (maya) and egoistic actions (karma) but are the same as Shiva in terms of essence and pure consciousness. When the cloud of ignorance is removed through the intervention of Shiva's grace (anugraha), a jiva becomes liberated and reunites with Shiva. Thereafter there will not be any difference between the two.

(v) Shiva as an Enlightened and Self-aware Entity

These are the various incarnations, emanations, divinities and deities and objectified energies that constitute the Shiva pantheon. They come into being as a projection of cosmic will during the various phases of creation. Some are manifested in the very beginning and some in the middle and some at the end. They perform many roles and implement the supreme will of Siva. Hanuman, Dakshinamurthy, Tandavamurthy, Bhairava, Virabhadra, Chandakesvara, Mahakaleswar, Ardhanariswara, Bhikshtanamurthy, Tandavamurthy are some of his well-known minor aspects or incarnations.

Some schools of Shaivism do not accept the concept of incarnations. According to them since Shiva is perfect being and creation is a manifestation of his dynamic will, there is no place for imperfection or disorder in his manifestation and so the questions of reincarnation to restore order does not arise. What we consider as his incarnations are but the embodiment of highly evolved jivas who come to the earth plane to help others on the path of liberation or perform specific tasks as willed by Siva.

(vi) Shiva as a Vedic deity

For those who do not practice pure Shaivism or any of the Shaiva schools, Shiva is a very popular god of Hindu or

Vedic pantheon and they worship him as such either as a personal god or in the company of other gods. An ancient god with pre-historic roots and far deeper antiquity than we can fathom, we find references to a god by the name Rudra in the Vedas. Rudra is the god of rain and thunder. In all probability when the vedic priests integrated different native traditions of India with the vedic traditions, they probably identified, Shiva, already a popular God of India, with the Rudra of the Vedas. Devout Hindus who practice mainstream Hinduism, indulge in devotional, ritualistic, ascetic, festive, yogic, musical and meditative practices to please Lord Shiva and attain his grace. As a personal god, Shiva has the qualities of a graceful and lovable god, who is easier to please and approach with love and devotion. As the lord of Kailash, he is an epitome of knowledge, humility and unconditional love. As a devoted husband, father and master, he bestows boons and unconditional love upon his beloved devotees. Whether they belong to the mainstream Shaivism or not, Hindus are very emotional and ecstatic about Lord Shiva, which can be seen and felt in many sacred places and temples of Shiva all over the country.

It is important to know that Lord Shiva is Brahman himself, who descends into lower planes to manifest himself in different aspects, which he does for his own ananda (pure joy). As deluded souls, it is important for us to know that each one of us is Shiva himself in human form and that we can by effort rediscover our own infinity. Shiva does not ask us to worship him, rather know ourselves as him only and live with that faith and conviction the rest of our lives.

4.15 112 Ways of Lord Shiva to Enhance Human Potential

Lord Shiva came to a dimension known as **Kaivalyapada**—where he offered 112 different ways in which a human being can attain to his fullest potential.

He declared, "If you use the human system, there are only 112 ways because there are only 112 doorways for this body through which it can attain." If you wish to do something, you can do something only with what you have on your hands. You cannot work with what is not on your hands.

Of these 112, 84 are purely 'kriya'. Fundamentally, 'kriya' means 'internal action'. When you do inner action, it does not involve the body and mind because both the body and mind are still external to you. When you have a certain mastery to do action with your energy, then it is a 'kriya'. But in today's world, most human beings do not have the necessary physical body to do Kriya Yoga in its entirety. It will just burn you down if you don't have the right kind of body. So, a combination that involves other aspects of you—body, mind and emotion—works best.

Besides the 84, the other ways also have aspects of 'kriya' because Adiyogi does not look at life through the intellect. He thinks human intellect is worth nothing. That's his opinion in the larger context of the existence, the human intellect is really nothing. Amongst ourselves, with our intellect and smart talk we can create little things, but in the larger existence, it doesn't mean anything.

Before you and me, something created all this. You can call it God, Shiva or whatever you want, but you didn't make it. If you look at any aspect of creation, one thing that it smacks of is intelligence—intelligence beyond your imagination. Intelligence and intellect are different things. For example, the body is an immensely complex chemical factory. There is a certain intelligence managing and conducting this. Do you believe that you could intellectually, logically conduct this whole factory? You would not be able to manage a single cell if you tried.

What you call 'intelligence' and what you refer to as 'creator' are not different. If you operate only within the limitations of your intellect, you will never know that which we refer to as the creator. You will just do the circus of life. Life is a circus when your intellect and body alone are involved. Life is a magical dance when the intelligence begins to play its role.

CHAPTER 5

Research on 'Om Namah Shivaya' Mantra

5.1 Om Namah Shivaya for Stress Management in Elderly Women with Hypertension

Paramahamsa Muktananda explained that "everyone can chant Om Namah Shivaya Mantra because: "This mantra is free of all restrictions. It can be repeated by anyone, young or old, rich or poor, and no matter what state a person is in, it will purify him/her". It was reported that by chanting Om Namah Shivaya mantra, it nullifies almost 99% of the negative impact of the planets. However, scientific evidence is lacking on this aspect.

In a study that was conducted at Sattva Cultural Space and Research Centre, Angamaly, Kerala, India, after obtaining institutional human ethical committee clearance, 8 elderly women aged 55-65 years with stage-2 hypertension were recruited in the present study. The following inclusion and exclusion criteria was used in recruiting the participants.

(i) Inclusion criteria:

- Willing women with stage-2 hypertension;
- Those on allopathic treatment for hypertension;
- Not suffering with any other disease or complications.

(ii) Exclusion criteria:

- Unwilling participants;
- Women with extreme blood pressure (BP) values;
- Those who already practicing any other alternative therapy.

All the participants were requested not to change their medication and life-style during the study. Participants acted as self-controls. Pre- and post- intervention scores were recorded by standard methods.

After recording baseline values, participants underwent practice sessions for 3 days under supervision of a yoga teacher from the centre. After the practice sessions, participants chanted Om Namah Shivaya for 108 times by using japa malā (rosary) with 108 beds at 6;30 in the morning for 40 days under supervision of a yoga teacher at the centre. All parameters were collected at 9:00 a.m. to prevent diurnal variations.

Depression Anxiety Stress Scale DASS- 42 was used to assess depression, anxiety and stress levels. Serum cortisol was also used to assess stress levels.

Assessment of autonomic functions: Blood pressure was recorded by using Diamond digital sphygmomanometer.

The Mini Mental State Examination (MMSE) was used to assess cognitive functions.

The results were expressed in terms of Mean±SD. Data was analyzed by SPSS 20.0. Paired t- test was used to compare the values of the groups. P value<0.05 was considered as significant.

The study provided preliminary scientific evidence for beneficial effects of "OM NAMAH SHIVAYA" chanting. Further detailed studies are recommended with more sample size and including both the genders to recommend inclusion of chanting in routine daily life style and also in clinical practice for the benefit of population in general.

5.2 Effect of Om Namah Shivaya Mantra on Neurons

Research published in 'Time' in which experiment was done to know how meditation works on mind and effect by which it increases concentration:

Researchers studied the 60 people which divided in 30-30 group. After experiments and study of these people, they found a correlation between meditation and the ability to focus, concentrate and remember. By chanting and meditation, brain significantly changed. As this happens when worshipping, and chanting this energetic mantra. Om Namah Shivaya meditation affects the brain at the molecular level due to chanting.

Science finds that our brain is made from neurons. Here's what science says: Neurons are made millions of connections to each other. Neurons interact with electric signals when brain processes to see, speak or hearing. Brainwork that allows concentration, remembering ability, the capability to understand and interpret by making the complex connection of neurons. The ability to remember or learn is not in full control of a human because it is incredibly difficult to make the brain more powerful to remember and increase capacity. But, the research finds the effect of meditation on this Mantra on the brain by diffusion tensor imaging and cortical thickness mapping. As there are many changes done by meditation brain structure and neuron construction, this proves the power of Om Namah Shivaya meditation and proof that mantra meditation works scientifically!

5.3 A Comparative Study of Frequencies of a Buddhist Mantra: 'Om Mani Padme Hum' and a Hindu mantra: 'Om Namah Shivaya'

Om Namah Shivaya is a holy salutation to Shiva. On the other hand, the most important mantra for the Tibetan Buddhists associated with the bodhisattva – Avalokiteshvara, is the six-syllable mantra "Om Mani Padme Hum". His Holiness, The 14th Dalai Lama of Tibet says, the six-syllable chant *Om Mani Padme Hum* is great but you need to think of each syllable when you chant it. The OM is an indivisible union of method and wisdom that can transform your impure body, speech, and mind into the pure exalted body, speech, and mind of a Buddha. MANI, the jewel, symbolizes the factors of method, compassion and love, the altruistic intention to become enlightened. PADME means lotus and symbolizes wisdom. Growing out of mud, but not being stained by mud, lotus indicates the quality of wisdom, which keeps you out of contradiction. The last syllable, Hum, means inseparability; symbolizing purity and can be achieved by the unity of method and wisdom.

This Buddhist mantra was studied in a research recently Avalokitesvara is regarded as a 'creator lord' with worlds found in the pores of his skin. The Karandavyuha Sutra is a text that is filled with techniques for folding these concepts. The Buddhist Mahayana definitely took on influences from the Shiva devotees at the time where there was a lot of interaction between the Buddhist and Hindus during the writing of these mantras and therefore there is a lot of similarity in the texts.

The sutras of the Pali era were more dedicated to the representation and working of the mind which is when devotion and mysticism was more popular. The Mahayana sutras were more directed to attain a transcendental experience and therefore very powerful. Study claims that the 'Om Mani Padme Hum' mantra is said to have originated from one of the Mahayana sutra i.e., Karandavyuha Sutra which apparently contains the manifestations and works of Avalokitesvara. Since this sutra has close affinities to non-Buddhist literature, the six syllable

mantra is said to have been conceptualized or evolved from 'Shiva's' five syllable mantra 'Om Namah Shivaya'.

From the electrons spinning around the nucleus of an atom, to the planets spinning around suns in the galaxy, everything is in movement. Everything is a vibration; a frequency. Mystics of the past and present have known that the whole universe is vibrating with energy and this energy vibrates at various frequencies., emotions, people and even planets differ from each other, and everything else, because of their unique vibrational frequency. Tuning the body to these frequencies can bring a phenomenal change in personality and this can be achieved by the frequencies generated from chants of mantras.

Meditation and healing practices that induce vibrations have provided us the secrets of resonance, which can induce several conformational changes in the patterns of consciousness. A living system may have many resonant frequencies due to their degrees of freedom, where each can vibrate as a harmonic oscillator supporting the progression of vibrations as waves that moves as a ripple within the whole system.

In a recent study, the frequencies of the 'Om Mani Padme Hum' chant were measured for each of the six syllables, where the frequencies within each of these syllables can possibly create a resonance effect, as a result of formation of constructive interference patterns between the frequencies of each syllable which may be the reason this chant exhibits a therapeutic/healing effect on the body and its functions. Chanting the 'Om Mani Padme Hum' mantra can actuate the frequencies associated with each syllable, to resonate at frequencies known to bring a change at a physical and biological level. Some of the frequencies measured in the study have been be used during several healing practices. This mantra has also shown enhanced cognitive effects in organisms without auditory apparatus where the interaction is assumed to be taking place at a cellular and biochemical level, which confirms the therapeutic effect of the frequencies associated with this chant at a cellular level.

This study evaluates the frequencies for both chants which seem to be correlated and therefore it is hypothecated that if their origins are from the similar source then there is a possibility of similarity in the frequencies and frequency patterns between these chants. Comparing the frequency patterns for these chants would help decipher the mystical and healing properties associated with these mantras and why they have been widely used for such purposes.

The chanting of the Tibetan meditational chant 'Om Mani Padme Hum' was inspired from the

soundtrack "Om Mani Padme Hum" by Tibetan Incantations (Nascente) while chanting of 'Om Namah Shivaya' was inspired from the soundtrack 'Aum Namah Shivaya' by 'Sounds of Isha'

(Vairagya-Bonding with Beyond). The chants were recorded during a regular chanting exercise using an in-built voice recorder in the Lenovo Ideatab. A1000-G tablet equipped with a 1.2 GHz dual-core Cortex A-9 processor (MediaTek 8317), 4GB RAM and an Android 4.1 Jelly Bean operating software. The chanting was performed in a semi-sound proof room, with more importance to the intonations of each syllable, such that the frequencies associated while reciting each syllable was crisp and clear. The recordings were saved as.mp3 files with a bit rate of 128 kbps to be processed later. An overall frequency analyses for these.mp3 files were done using the WavePad NCH software Version 6.18, which uses a FFT analytical tool to determine the actual frequency recordings of the soundtrack. These.mp3 files were further snipped using the Audacity version 2.1.2 software, where the soundtrack was split into six syllables for the Tibetan chant and five syllables for the Hindu chant using an online audio splitter software – Song Cutter by Mediafox Marketing. Each of the.mp3 files were replicated and joined using the Helium Audio Joiner by Imploded Software, to make a lengthier soundtrack i.e., approximately 5 mins each for every syllable for better analysis.

The analysis for each soundtrack was carried out in a semi-sound proof environment, where the generated.mp3 files for each syllable was played on an I-ball Tarang 2.1 music system with one subwoofer (20 watts RMS max) and two satellite speakers (10 watts RMS max each) with a total output of 40 watts RMS max and frequency ranges for – woofer as 20Hz -200Hz and satellites as 100Hz-20kHz at a decibel output range of 75 – 80 db. The frequencies for each syllable were analysed on three android based applications – Spectrum Analyzer by Raspberrywood Version 5.0.3, Spectrum Analyzer by Keuwlsoft Version 1.3 and Sound Analyzer by Tinia Soft Version 1.02 using a Lenovo Ideatab A1000-G tablet with a 1.2 GHz dual-core Cortex A-9 processor (MediaTek 8317), a 4GB RAM with an Android 4.1 Jelly Bean operating software. The frequencies for each syllable were analysed by the android applications

with an FFT analytical tool of Hz against the decibel output value. By comparing the frequencies recorded for each syllable by all three applications, a final set of frequencies for each syllable was confirmed. Besides, the high decibel frequencies considered for the study, there were several other background frequencies which were observed, but since they were at very low decibel ranges, they were not considered as part of the final set of frequencies. The comparative results for each of the android applications for the 'Om Mani Padme Hum' and that for each of the android applications for the 'Om Namah Shivaya' mantra was carried out in this study.

The syllable OM is common for both these chants but based on its pronunciation while chanting, the frequencies that emerge are different for each of them. Lower frequencies such as 99.3 Hz, 106.47Hz and 126 Hz are part of the frequencies of the gamma waves recorded in the brain and, therefore, can stimulate gamma brainwave entrainment. Brain wave entrainment, sometimes referred to as binaural beat is a popular way of inducing desired mental states and accessing our untapped potential. Binaural beats are aural tones played at different frequencies in each ear. Chanting the OM in these mantras has a direct impact with the gamma wave patterns of the brain which have showed increased mental activity/ cognitive enhancement, freedom from distractibility, high levels of info-processing, learning and focus, high short-term memory ability and migraine prevention. EEG recordings of skilled Buddhist monks with years of training have shown a significant rise in gamma wave activity in the 80-120 Hz range while this effect was lower in new meditators. For these Buddhist monks, the purpose of meditation is to free oneself from suffering and gain spiritual liberation which is the same reason for meditative practice in other religions.

Buddhist teachings claim that by chanting the OM syllable, an impure body, speech and mind can be transformed into pure ones of a Buddha, who was once impure and later by removing negative attributes, achieved enlightenment on his path. Based on the comparison of frequencies for both the chants and their syllables, there is a resilient similarity in the frequency patterns for each of the syllables and therefore there seems to be some commonality in the experience and healing capability of these chants. 126 Hz was the most common frequency for all the syllables in both chants. 126 Hz is also part of the gamma wave frequency patterns in the brain and therefore when induced, it can enhance the gamma wave activity in the brain. The frequencies associated with these chants and their syllables are the most important as there is a direct effect of these frequencies on the brain. The final grouping and comparison of the frequencies for the syllables of the two mantras have shown some common frequencies which have apparently been used by healers and meditators to bring a significant change in the lives of individuals.

Ancient Egyptians used Solfeggio scale for healing and altering consciousness in large sound chambers where they would play frequencies at 528 Hz throughout the chambers to generate specific effects on individuals, which is also a frequency found in both mantras and in most of the syllables. This frequency is also known to increase energy, clarity of mind, awareness, awakened or activated creativity, ecstatic states like deep inner peace, dance and celebration and activate one's imagination, intention and intuition. 800 - 825 Hz range of frequencies is linked to the ability to see through the illusions of one's life and has been used in healing techniques to open up a person for communication with the awareness of the spiritual order. For cellular processes, this frequency is known to support the cell to transform itself into a system of higher level. 639 Hz frequency has been used by healers and meditators on individuals to enhance communication, understanding, tolerance and love. Healers call this frequency as Relationship Harmonization where they claim that the frequency results in complete healing radiant light that descends upon the listener filling the personal mind with the influences of balance, health and tranquillity, which is also common in some of the syllable of both chants.

In conclusion, it has been observed in this research study that both the mantras: 'Om Mani Padme Hum' and 'Om Namah

Shivaya' create the same effect in the brain, leading to calmness and enhancement of cognitive capabilities.

It is once again recommended that more research work is needed on this powerful mantra: 'Om Namah Shivaya'.

CHAPTER 6

Om Namah Shivaya-Based Meditation (Japa)

Many meditators have made the 'Om Namah Shivaya' mantra a part of their daily routine. There are no restrictions as to who may learn and practice the mantra, nor is it necessary to embrace the mythology surrounding the mantra in order to use it. It is enough to approach it with respect. The first step is to learn to recite the mantra correctly. Including 'OM', it has only six syllables and it can be learned very easily. Slow repetition combined with a review of the meaning of each word will help in appreciating its significance. Once the mantra is learned, bring it to mind as you begin your daily meditation, as a kind of invocation to your normal practice. After calming the body and breath, do 9, 18, 36, or even 108 recitations, and allow your mind to become absorbed in the sounds and rhythm of each line.

Let the mantra draw your awareness to the centre of the heart or the point between eyebrows, whichever feels natural to you, and use that centre as the focal point of your awareness. If you are reciting the mantra to help with a health problem, focus your awareness at the navel centre. At some point you may wish to do more repetitions in a given period of time. There are many reasons for wanting to do this. You may be going through a period of poor health or low energy; you may be seeking a deeper sense of security or confidence; you may feel stressed or overwhelmed by events or attachments in your life; the death of someone for whom you are dedicating your practice, may be approaching. But often the sentiments that draw one to this practice are prompted less by health issues than by a deep urge to be a part of the unfolding harmony of life itself. The nurturing quality of the mantra acts in the human mind and heart just as the forces of light, water, and soil act in the life of a plant. The mantra magnifies the qualities of personality that give our lives the purpose and meaning.

6.1 Chanting (Japa) of Om Namah Shivaya Mantra

Japa is a special science. It is the science of going into the deeper layers of mind which progressively become of a higher and yet higher frequency. It is a science of devoting the mind's energies to a specific goal so that the particular divine conscious forces may arise within us and make us their dwelling place. Through whichever deities' *japa* you perform, the qualities, the attributes of that *devata* (deity) enters into you. What is a *devata*? The pictures and images are not the *devata*. *Devas* are conscious, living forces. We give them bodies because we project those forms onto them. In the *mantra vidya* (mantra science), we think of the *mantra* as the body of the *devata*. A *Devata* has two forms, a *jyoti* form and a *nada* form. There is the universal conscious sound, the *Maha Nada* of the cosmos, and certain waves of that cosmos are the *mantras*. These mantras have been revealed in the "minds" of the rishis.

Use a mala (a rosary, a string of 108 beads) to keep track of your practice. Treat one complete mala as 100 repetitions of the mantra. A fulfilling practice is to complete 8,000 repetitions in 40 days. This can be accomplished by doing one mala in the morning and one in the evening. Each day, before beginning, remember the seer of the Om Namah Shivaya, the Lord Shiva. Simply bring his spirit to mind, paying respect to him. Then begin your practice. In the course of time, you may find that the one or two malas you do each day have become a regular element of your life.

In the beginning of reciting a *mantra* we always remember the *rishi* of that *mantra*. For example, the *rishi* of *Gayatri* is Vishvamitra to whom the *mantra* was revealed Om Namah Shivaya mantra is Shiva's form and will settle people into their ultimate goal: *moksha* (liberation). You may say that one does not want to think that far about *moksha*; however, liberation and enlightenment do not come dramatically; they come in tiny little steps. When one knot of one's character, of one's psychology, is loosened, one small step is taken toward liberation. We are unable to loosen that knot. So a prayer for *moksha* is a prayer for loosening our immediate knots. In the practice of *japa*, which *mantra* should be done, by whom, at what time of life? When a *mantra diksha* (mantra initiation) is given, the guru has taught the student-initiator (*dikshata*) to observe the personality and let the *mantra* be transmitted.

6.2 Methods of Chanting Mantra

6.2.1 Baikhari (Audible)

By chanting aloud which can be heard easily is called "Baikhari" Chanting.

6.2.1.1 Advantages of Baikhari Chanting:

- Removes thoughts
- Easy conceptualization of thoughts
- Makes meditation easy

6.2.2 Upanshu (whispering)

Chanting of mantra in low voice, or just whispering so that only practitioner can understand is called "Upanshu" Chanting.

6.2.2.1 Advantages of "Upanshu":

- Long duration chanting (8 to 10 hours)
- Purposeful Mantra repetition (for wealth, health, happiness etc.)
- Destiny Errors can be corrected with this type of chanting

6.2.3 Manasik (Mental)

Without chanting aloud or whispering, mantra is repeated in mind, this type of mantra chanting is difficult and can be learnt only with practice.

6.2.3.1 Advantages of Mental Chanting:

- Subtle form of chanting
- Commonly used by advance practitioners
- Leads to higher states of awareness

6.3 Some Guidelines for Om Namah Shivaya Mantra-Based Meditation/Japa

6.3.1 At What Time Should One Perform the 'Om Namah-Shivaya' Meditation (Sadhana)?

'Om Namah-Shivaya' Meditation is also known as ***Sandhyopasana or Sandhya Vandana,*** which means meditation which is performed at dawn and dusk every day. *Sandhya* means the meeting period of day and night. *Upasana* means meditation. Thus *Sandhyopasana* means the meditation during early morning and early evening. The deity of this mantra is Lord Shiva. By meditating on the brilliance of early morning sun our intellect can be sharpened. The early morning and early evening periods are considered as the periods of peace or the moments of spiritual power. Some sadhakas (practitioners of meditation) practice this sadhana three times a day, that is, early morning (approximately two hours before the sunrise), noon time (when the sun is vertically above you and the dusk time (approximately one hour after the sunset). Thus this Mantra Upasana or spiritual contemplation should be performed thrice a day at the conjunction (sandhi) times, (i) sandhi of the night and the dawn (Purvahna), (ii) sandhi of the forenoon and afternoon (Madhyahna), and (iii) the sandhi of evening (sunset) and night (Sayahna). If this is not possible under some circumstances, it should be done in the mornings and evenings at least. As such, one can do this Mantra-chanting many time in a day, at least mentally.

Doing sandhya-upasana every day with the japa (rhythmic chanting) of this Mantra is said to bestow longevity, strength, intelligence, success, glory and spiritual light. Upasana provides sublime food for soul.

The "Chanakya Niti" highlights this as:

Vipro Vraaksastasya Mulam Cha Sandhya, Vedah Sakha Dharmakarmani Patram |
Tasyanmulam Yatna Na Raksaniyam, Chinne Mule Naiva Sakha Na Patram ||

– *Chanakya Niti ||10-13||*

Meaning: Sandhya (upasana) is the root of the tree of (healthy, hearty and enlightened) life. The Vedas (that is, the source of righteous knowledge) constitute its branches and religious activities are its leaves. Blossoming growth of a tree is dependent on the life of its roots. Without the roots there will be no possibility of any branch or leaves. In essence, the above shloka (likewise many guidelines in the Shastra Literature), conveys that sandhya (upasana) is the basis of human life in the truest sense.

When time is a problem, it can be practiced at any time of the day but at least one to two hours after having any meals. It is more effective when performed before taking any meals. "Sins committed consciously or unconsciously during the day are neutralized by the evening meditation and those of the night are reduced to ash by the morning meditation", says Manu Smriti. The Sandhya meditation that is done before sunrise, while the stars are still visible (Brahma Muhurat) is the best time. Similarly, the meditation in the evening between the time of sunset up to an hour after the sunset are good time for meditation. Besides this, the best time for meditation is when one's heart is filled with the love for God Almighty. As the Upasana is done at the conjunction (sandhi) time, it is also called Sandhya-Upasana. It is also called Sandhya-Vandana (adoration or worship) or simply Sandhya.

Sandhau sandhya mupaseet.

– Gautama Maharishi

Meaning: The sandhya upasana or worship, ought to be performed at the sandhi time, the confluence!!

Ajyotisho darshanat sandhih, jyotishi bhanutare.
sajyotishya jyotisho darshanadvagyatah.

Meaning: When the Sun and the Stars are visible together is the time of sandhi, the confluence; sandhya has to be performed at such time.

Ahoratrasya Ya Sandhih Suryanaksatra Varjita |
Satu Sandhya Samakhyata Munibhistatva Darsibhih ||

– Ayurvedic treatise "Sahityika Subhashita Vaidyakam"

Meaning: Around the times of sunrise and sunset when neither sun nor any of the stars are seen even in the clear sky.) These time intervals (sandhya-times) are described as extremely sensitive with respect to the effect on bodily, mental and spiritual wellbeing. We should be very careful about what we do in this period.

- So the best time to chant is early morning hours (Brahma Muhurta), around 4.00AM, or at least one hour before the sunrise.
- Make it a practice to chant at least 3 times before you start driving.

- For prosperity, Om Namah Shivaya Mantra should be chanted while facing the east for at least 108 times in a row.

Before chanting, you can fill a glass of water, place it before you as you cover it with the right palm, chant this mantra for the required times and sprinkle the water all around the house for prosperity.

6.4 Japa by Rudraksha Mala

It is recommended that for a better focus, the mantra japa (chanting) should be done by holding the Rudraksha Mala (with 108 beads plus one Guru bead) in the right hand and counting one bead per mantra chanting.

6.4.1 About Rudraksha Beads

In Sanskrit language, Rudra is another name for Lord Shiva and aksha means "teardrops", so Rudraksha can be translated as "teardrops of Shiva". According to Vedic Scriptures, Shiva once went into deep meditation for the well-being of all living creatures. When he woke up, tear drops welled down from his eyes on realizing the suffering of living creatures. On reaching the earth, these tears took the form of seeds that germinated into Rudraksha trees (Elaeocarpus ganitrus). The dry seeds from this tree form the sacred Rudraksha beads. The eye of Rudra (Shiva is considered to be the most potent manifestation of the Cosmic Force. Hence, the Rudraksha is the object of veneration and also the source to reach the higher self. Rudraksha is often believed to symbolize the link between the earth and the heaven.

Rudraksha is the seed of a particular tree species which usually grows at a certain altitude in the mountains – mainly in the Himalayan region. Today, they are mostly found in Nepal, Burma, Thailand or Indonesia. They are there in some parts of the Western Ghats in South India, but the best quality ones come from a certain altitude in Himalayas because somehow the soil, atmosphere, and everything influences it. These seeds have a very unique vibration.

Elaeocarpus ganitrus grows in the area from the Gangetic plain in the foothills of the Himalayas to Southeast Asia, Nepal, Indonesia, New Guinea to Australia, Guam, and Hawaii. Rudraksha seeds are covered by an outer husk of blue when fully ripe, and for this reason are also known as blueberry beads. The blue colour is not derived from pigment but is structural. It is an evergreen tree that grows quickly. The Rudraksha tree starts bearing fruit in three to four years from germination. As the tree matures, the roots form buttresses, rising up near the trunk and radiating out along the surface of the ground.

According to ancient Vedic texts, these beads are endowed with cosmic powers to elevate the soul and assist on the path of ascension. Shiva himself is always portrayed wearing a Rudraksha beads Mala on his head, arms and hands.

Medicinally they are known to: heal many of the mind & body ailments, by cooling when worn against the skin, reduce heart disease and lower blood pressure, increase mental clarity, memory & general awareness, calm the central nervous system, quiet the mind & free one from negative thoughts, increase immunity, energy & stamina, and rejuvenate the entire mind & body.

Extensive scientific research has been conducted over the years by leading scientists in universities in India, and now also in the west. Their findings have proven that Rudraksha beads have certain electrical and magnetic properties, and when worn against the skin, and especially over the heart, act on our human neural network in a number of beneficial ways. It can balance the heart's magnetic field, control pulse rate, improve blood circulation, and purify the blood. When we wear Rudraksha beads we are literally carrying sacks of oxygen, carbon and hydrogen against our bodies as we soak up the vibration of these pure living organisms. Rudraksha beads also increase negative ion levels and act directly on our central nervous system, by releasing certain chemicals in our bodies that are responsible for positive emotions and a calm mind. Many people for this reason alone have found freedom from stress, depression and lethargy when using Rudraksha beads. Rudraksha beads are also said to absorb and store solar energy, and thus releases and distributes this solar power into all parts of the body.

6.4.2 Ek mukhi, Panchmukhi Rudraksha Beads

The number of faces a bead can have varies from a single face up to 21 faces. They are used for different purposes, so it would be improper to just buy something in the shop and put it on the body. Wearing the wrong type could disturb one's life. A lot of people want to wear an *ek mukhi*, which has only one face because it is very powerful. You yourself have many faces. When you have many faces, if you wear an ek mukhi, you are asking for trouble. *Five-faced beads or Panchmukhi* is safe and good for everyone – man, woman and child. It is for general well-being, health and freedom. It lowers your blood pressure, calms your nerves and brings a certain calmness and alertness in your nervous system. Children below 12 years of age can wear six-faced beads. It will help them calm down and be more focused. Above all they will receive the right type of attention from the adult.

6.4.3 About Rudraksha Mala

Usually the beads are strung together as a *mala (rosary).* Traditionally, they believe the number of beads is 108 plus one. The extra bead is the bindu. There must always be a bindu to the mala, otherwise the energy becomes cyclical and people who are sensitive may become dizzy. When you string them, it is best that they are strung with either a silk thread or a cotton thread. If you wear it with a thread then it is good to take care to change the thread every six months. The mala can be worn all the time.

All the meditators, saints and sages always carry their mala wherever they go as these personalities ardently devote themselves to mantra japa meditation. Regular practice of Japa meditation incorporates the use of a mala that acts as a meditation aid. A traditional mala, as ours, has 108 beads, for keeping the count during meditation. Mala actually helps you focus or concentrate on the mantra you are chanting, so it keeps the mind focused and your attention drawn to the sound of the mantra. In this way, you will be able to enter a deeper meditation state and unwanted thoughts or distractions cease to unsettle your mind.

6.4.4 Benefits of Chanting Through Rudraksha Mala

By meditating with a Rudraksha beads mala or by wearing Rudraksha seeds against the skin it is believed to:

- increase the ability to focus,
- give clarity and peace of mind,
- improve memory,
- relieve stress and anxiety,
- increase stamina,
- strengthen the heart,
- balance the nervous system,
- bestow divine protection,
- increase abundance and prosperity.

There is no mantra, other than Om Namah Shivaya, as powerful as this for giving siddhi, desired results, and destroying enemies. It should not be given to the foolish, to the undisciplined, to those not on the path, to the bad, or those fettered by the five kleshas. This alone is the very blissful thing destroying enemies. This mantra ls the powerful King of Mantras, giving the fruit of inituation, like the wish-fulfilling tree. Unless one previously prepares this King of Mantra it does not grant success, therefore one should prepare the mantra using methods indicated by the Guru. Only those who obtain this method from the Guru's hand should do this preparation.

This powerful King of Mantras is greater than the Aeon Tree! One should prepare it 400,000 times, or half that, O Maheshvari. One should never perform this method less than 100,000 times. One should give a tenth of recitation, a tenth of homa, a tenth oblation, a tenth sprinkling, and a tenth feeding. All this the sadhaka should do if he wishes to prepare the mantra. O Ishvari, one should give dakshina to the Guru as necessary.

6.5 Om Namah Shivaya Mantra Homam/ Havan/Yagya

6.5.1 Procedure for Om Namah Shivaya Havan

Here is the procedure to perform the Om Namah Shivaya Havan/Yagya. Anyone can do this at home daily at least once (at dawn) or twice (dawn and dusk).

6.5.1.1 Timing: Morning before sunrise and evening before sunset.

6.5.1.2 Required Items:

Copper Havan kund, small size, which is easily available.

(a) Samagri required for Ahuti:-

i. Black Sesame (kaala Til)

ii. Jiggery (Gud)

iii. Jau

iv. Rice (Chawal)

v. Cow Ghee (Desi Ghee)

Mix all the above Ahuthi Samagri and store it or you can prepare as much as required daily before doing Havan.

(b) Samagri for Havan:-

i. Gobbar Kand (Dried Cow Dung cake).

ii. Mango or pipal tree sticks dried.

iii. Karpooram (Camphor)

6.5.1.3 Method For Havan:-

Invoke Maa Sanjeevani Shakti and Start the Havan.

Take one Marble Tile or any other Kota tile and place Havan Kund and place the Gobar kand (Cow Dung Cake) and one Karpooram (Camphor) on it and then place Mango or Pipal tree sticks (straight wooden pieces) in it, as required and then again put 2-3 Karpooram pieces and light fire to it. When it starts burning completely, give Ahuthi 11 times or 21 times or 108 times of Samagri mentioned above by your three fingers.

The Divine Havan arises in the form of smoke and fire and makes the whole home and everyone 100% healthy and positive, not only you and your home but everyone near you and your area. It is also useful for the person suffering from brain haemorrhage, terminal illness etc. and it activates all body cells and creates new cells.

6.6 Abhisheka: Shiva Puja

Abhisheka is a part of Shiva Puja. Without Abhisheka, worship of Shiva is incomplete. During Abhisheka Rudra, Purushasukta, Chamaka, ***Om Namah Shivaya*** Japa, etc., are chanted in a particular rhythm and order. Monday is very important day for Lord Siva and the thirteenth day of the fortnight (Pradosha) is very sacred. On these days, devotees of Shiva worship Him with special Puja, Abhisheka with Ekadasa-Rudra, Archana, offering plenty of Prasad, and illumination.

Lord Shiva is worshipped in His Saguna aspect in the form of Shiva lingam. Generally Shiva-bhaktas do Panchayatana Puja. In this Puja, Lord Shiva, Ganesha, Parvati, Suryanarayana and Shaligram are duly worshipped. Worship the Lord daily with all sincerity and faith. You will have all wealth, peace of mind, attainment of Dharma, Artha, Kama and Moksha also. You will lead a prosperous life and enter the immortal abode of Shiva-Sayujya, on death.

Lord Shiva is fond of Abhishekam. In Shiva temples, a pot made up of copper or brass with a hole in the center is kept hanging over the image or Ling of Shiva, and water falls on the image throughout day and night. Pouring over the Linga, water, milk, ghee, curd, honey, cocoanut water, Panchaamrit, etc, is called Abhishekam. Abhishekam is done for Lord Shiva. Rudram is chanted along with the Abhishekam. Shiva is propitiated by Abhishekam.

Shiva drank the poison that emanated from the churning of the ocean of milk and wore the Ganga and the Moon on his head to cool His head. Shiva has the fiery third eye. Constant Abhishekam cools this eye too.

The greatest and the highest Abhishekam is to pour the waters of pure love on the Aatm Linga of the lotus of the heart. The external Abhishekam with various objects will help the growth of devotion and adoration for Shiva and eventually lead to internal Abhishekam with pure abundant flow of love.

In Ekaadash-Rudram Abhishek, every Rudram is chanted with distinctive articles for Abhishek. Ganga water, milk, ghee, honey, rose-water, coconut water, sandal paste, Panchaamrit, scented oil, sugarcane juice and lime juice are made use of for Abhishekam. After every Abhishek, pure water is poured over the head of Shiva Ling. When Rudra is recited only once, the different articles of Abhishek are made use of after every stanza of the Rudram. The Abhishekam water or other articles used for

Abhishekam are considered very sacred and bestow immense benefits on the devotees who take it as the Lord's Prasad. It purifies the heart and destroys countless sins. You must take it with intense Bhaava and faith.

A devotee should be regular in doing Abhishekam for the Lord. He should get Rudram and Chamakam by heart. Ekaadash Rudra is more powerful and effective. In Northern India, every man or woman takes a lot of water and pours it on the image of Shiv. This also causes beneficial results and brings about the fulfilment of one's desire. Abhishekam on Shiva Raatri day is very effective.

May you all recite Rudra Path which describes the glory of Shiva and his manifestations in every living being, in every animate and inanimate being. May you do Shiva Abhishekam daily and thus obtain the grace of Lord Shiva.

6.6.1 Legend About Shiva Abhishekam

Story goes that after the Creation was complete, Lord Shiva began to live on top of the mount Kailash with his consort Parvati. One day Parvati asked Shiva that his devotees perform many rituals to please the Lord, but which one pleases him the most. To this, Shiva replied that on the 14th night of the new moon, during the month of Phalguna is his favourite day. The day is celebrated as Shiva Ratri. On this day, devotees observe strict spiritual discipline and worship Shiva in four different forms during each of the four successive three-hour periods of the night. Shiva further said that the devotees offer him Bel leaves (Bilva Patra) on that day and that those leaves were precious to him than the precious jewels and flowers. Explaining the right way of worshipping Shiva, the Lord said, devotees should bathe me in the milk during the first period, in curd at the second, in clarified butter in the third and in honey in the fourth and the last period. Shiva further added that next morning devotees must feed the Brahmanas first and, only after following the prescribed ritual must they break the fast. Shiva further told Parvati that rituals of Shiva Ratri could not be compared with any other performed for him.

Parvati Devi became deeply impressed with Shiva's speech and she narrated it to her friends. Through them the word spread all over the creation. Hence Shiva devotees began to celebrate Shiva Ratri by fasting and by performing the ceremonial baths and making an offering of Bel leaves.

6.6.2 Rituals Along with Mantras

Following are the ***ritualistic steps*** for Abhishekam:

Sprinkle water over yourself and all items of Puja chanting.

Om Apavitrah Pavitro Va Sarva Vastan Gatopi Va
Yah Smaret Pundari Kaksham Sa Bahya Bhyantarah Shuchi.

Meaning: May all things unholy become holy, may all lower tendencies depart, just as soon as we transcend may within and without be purified!

Then Chant:

"Om Gurubhyo Namaha
Om Ganeshaya Namaha
Om Kula Devatabhyo Namaha
Om Ishta Devatabhyo Namaha
Om Mata Pitribhyam Namaha"

Meaning: I bow to guru, I bow to Ganesha, I bow to the family deity, I bow to my personal deity, I bow to my parents

Place water on right hand with spoon of Achamani and sip after each of these 3 mantras

"Om Keshavaya Namaha
Om Narayana Namaha
Om Madhavaya Namaha"

Place water on right hand and pour on ground:

"Om Govindaya Namaha"

Do three short rounds of pranayama breaths.

"Om Pranavasya Parabrahma Rishihi Paramatma Devata
Daivi Gayatri Chandaha
Pranayamae Viniyogaha"

Bathe lingam with water and then all Abhisheka liquids one by one. Then bathe Him with Punchamrit and again with water. All this while chant Om Namah Shivaya or the Shiva Moola Mantra. Wipe Him and place Him on Pedestal.

Now chant Sadyojaat mantra:

Om Sadyojaatam Prapadyaami Sadyojataajava Namo Namaha Bhave Bhavenaati Bhave Bhavasvamaam Bhavodbhavay Namaha

Offer Sandal Paste making a Tripunda on His Western Face with Vamadeva mantra:

Om Vamdevaya Namah, Jyeshthaay Namah, Shreshthay Namah, Rudraay Namah, Kaalay Namah,Kala Vikarannaay Namah, Bal Vikaranaay Namah, Balaay Namah Bala

Pramathanaay Namah, Sarva Bhoot Damanaay Namah, Manomanaay Namah.

Offer dhoop and incense to Him with mantra below:

"Om Aghorebhyo Ghorebhyo Ghor Tarebhayaha Sarvebhya Sarva Sharvvebhyo Namaste Astu Rudra Roopebhyaha"

Offer flowers with mantra below:

"Om Tatpurushaaya Vidmahe Mahadevaay Dheemahi Tanno Rudraha Prachodayaat"

Chant Eeeshan mantra:

Om Eeshaanah Sarvavidyaanam Eeshwar Sarvabhootaanaam Brahmaadipati Brahmanaadhipati Brahma Shivome Astu Sadaa Shivom

Invocation: *Avahanam Samarpayami Sri Shiva Maha Devaya Charana Kamalebhyo Namaha*

Seat: *Asanam Samarpayami Sri Shiva Maha Devaya Charana Kamalebhyo Namaha*

Cloth: *Vastram Samarpayami Sri Shiva Maha Devaya Charana Kamalebhyo Namaha*

Sandalwood or scent: *Chandanam Samarpayami Sri Shiva Maha Devaya Charana Kamalebhyo Namaha*

Rice: *Akshatan Samarpayami Sri Shiva Maha Devaya Charana Kamalebhyo Namaha*

Flower: *Pushpam Samarpayami Sri Shiva Maha Devaya Charana Kamalebhyo Namaha*

Dhoop: *Dhupam Samarpayami Sri Shiva Maha Devaya Charana Kamalebhyo Namaha*

Ghee lamp: *Deepam Samarpayami Sri Shiva Maha Devaya Charana Kamalebhyo Namaha*

Water drinking: *Achamaniyam Samarpayami Sri Shiva Maha Devaya Charana Kamalebhyo Namaha*

Fruit: *Naivedyam Samarpayami Sri Shiva Maha Devaya Charana Kamalebhyo Namaha*

Water drinking: *Achamaniyam Samarpayami Sri Shiva Maha Devaya Charana Kamalebhyo Namaha*

Betel nut – Paan: *Tambulam Samarpayami Sri Shiva Maha Devaya Charana Kamalebhyo Namaha*

Coconut: *Shri Phalam Samarpayami Sri Shiva Maha Devaya Charana Kamalebhyo Namaha*

Burn Camphor and offer to Him.

Karpura Shivam Karuna Vataram Samsara Saram Bhujagendraharam
Sada Vasantam Hridaya Ravinde Bhavam Bhavani Sahitam Namami

Chant Gayatri mantra 3 times:

Om Bhur Bhuvah Swaha
Om Tat Savitur Varenyum Bhargo Devasya Dhimahi Dhiyo Yonaha Prachodayat

Chant Surya mantra 3 times

Om Bhu Om Bhuvaha Om Swaha Om Maha Om Janaha Om Tapaha Om Satyam

Repeat and touch each after each mantra, right eye, left eye, forehead

Om Apo Jyothi Raso Amtritam
Brahma Bhu Bhuvaha Swarom

Chant Om Namah Shivaya mantra 108 times with Rudraksha mala.

Om Haum Joom Sah,Om Bhur Bhuvaha Swaha
Om Triambakam Yajamahey,Sungandhim Pushti Vardanam
Urvar Ukamiva Bandhanan,Mrityor Muksheeya Mamritat
Om Swaha Bhuvaha Bhu Om Sah Joom Haum Om

Bow or supplicate, then chant this last prayer:

Om Purnamada purnamidam purnath purnamudyachite
Purnasya purnamadaya purna mevaya shishyate

6.6.3 Benefits for the Materials Used for Abhishekam

The material list includes pure water, milk, sugarcane juice, lemon juice, ghee, honey, waters of sacred rivers, sea water, Kush water, rice powder, cooked rice, Panchaamrit, Panchgavya.

- Milk gives long life, freedom from diseases, and for begetting a son. It is believed that by doing Abhishek with milk, even a barren woman begets children.
- Ghee gives Moksha state
- Curd gives good children
- Honey gives melodious voice
- Rice powder frees from debts

- Sugar cane juice gives good health
- Panchaamrit gives wealth
- Lemon juice removes fear of death
- Sugar cane juice gives good health and removes enmity
- Tender coconut water gives enjoyment
- Cooked Rice (Annam) gives majestic life
- Sandal gives Lakshmi's grace
- Water Abhishek gives rain.
- Kush water Abhishekam – becomes free from all diseases.
- Sacred water gives Moksha
- Ghee, honey and sugarcane juice give wealth,
- Bilva Patra and flowers should be offered in Shiv Puja.

6.7 How is Mantra Introduced by the Guru to His Disciple?

How are these mantras revealed? In the beginning one letter is revealed to the rishi. It is the first letter of the mantra, for instance, the sound 'Om'. For days together the disciple just listens to that sound. He comes out of meditation and the next morning again he sits, goes inside and follows that sound. Ultimately the sound expresses itself in the form of a mantra, for instance, the bija mantra: **'Om Namah Shivaya'.**

There are special mantras called bija mantra or seed mantras. These are Aim, Hrim, Klim, Shreem, Hrom, Om, etc. These bija mantras are elaborated on by the Guru, they are developed like you develop a photograph. **'Om Namah Shivaya'** is a fire mantra.

When a disciple accepts a mantra from his Guru, he is establishing a relationship with the Guru, and he is also receiving a sound of great power. A personal mantra is one of the most precious things in life. Getting a mantra from a Guru is very different from reading a mantra, knowing about the mantra, discovering a mantra, or getting all the knowledge about the mantra from a book. When a Guru says, **"Om Namah Shivaya"**, he is sending energy. I'm sending you energy. Speech is energy. Sound is energy. It is a current, it is a wave, it is a frequency, it is a velocity. It has electrons and protons. Many things. So, when the Guru says, **"Om Namah Shivaya"** in your ears, it is completely different from the knowledge which you get from the book.

The sound enters when the Guru whispers the mantra, and immediately they put a cloth on the disciple. Now, when the Guru whispers a mantra, it is called Upanshu. That is how the mantra is given to the disciple. And that mantra has to be repeated. The Guru says to do it in the morning the first thing after you leave your bed. After accepting the mantra, you become the disciple. When you practice that mantra you strengthen the Guru-disciple relationship and once this is established, you can become the channel through which the Guru's thoughts are conducted. The disciple must be regular in his meditation. If there is regular contact with the Guru, you can draw upon his unconscious help and guidance. In this way maximum benefits are derived from the sadhana.

6.8 Breath Awareness

Become aware of the breath, the natural breath which moves at the speed of about fifteen rounds per minute. The breath has to be felt at the nosetip, flowing through both the nasal orifices. Then synchronise your mantra with the natural flow of the breath, either one mantra with inspiration and one with exhalation, or more than one mantra with inspiration and exhalation. The number of mantras per breath depends both upon the length of your mantra, and on your comfort level.

6.8.1 The Flow of Breath

When you practice japa, your breath must always be flowing from the left nostril. If the breath is flowing through both nostrils, that is alright, but the right alone should not be flowing. If the breath is not flowing through the left nostril, then there is a simple method of changing the flow from the right to the left. In ancient times they used a special kind of staff or armrest. It was made of wood and was placed under the right armpit. A slight pressure was applied under the armpit. After a short period of time, the air stops flowing through the right nostril and starts to flow through the left nostril. This is a traditional method of swara yoga. There is a simpler method. Place your left hand into the centre of the right armpit and apply some light pressure. You will soon find that the breath will start to flow through the left nostril.

6.9 Mantra Anushthana

Anushthana is a traditional practice in which a particular mantra is chanted for a prescribed number of times. A Sankalpa or vow has to be made to complete them over a given time period. There are many kinds of anushtan but the two most important are Sadharana Anushthana and purashcharana Anushthana. Sadharana Anushthana is done on all nine days of Navaratri. During this time, simple, bland food is taken and no work is done. Purascharana is a long Anushthana in which the mantra is repeated as many hundreds of thousands of times as the number of matras or letters it contains. For example, if the mantra is **Om Namah Shivaya**, it must be repeated 500,000 times – this means 5000 malas. This can be completed in a short period of time or over a long period at your convenience. If you do not want to undertake the full number, then you can do only half or one quarter. Anushthana is typically initiated on an auspicious day, for example, the day of an eclipse.

6.10 Don't Fight with Yourself

Sit for one hour, try for two hours, and try to extend the time so that eventually you can sit for three hours. Sit down properly – **Om Namah Shivaya… Om Namah Shivaya… Om Namah Shivaya…** You begin to think about your job… **Om Namah Shivaya**… Oh my mind is so restless, I'd better do some pranayama… No, I am too tired…

Okay. You see, this is what you have been doing all the while, wrestling with yourself, with your mind. Who is controlling whom? You are fighting with yourself. The right hand is pulling the left hand, the left hand is pulling the right. The entire atmosphere of antagonism is self-created. You are creating a split in your own mind. One part of the mind is fighting with another part of the mind. One tendency of the mind is fighting with another tendency of the same mind. Therefore, when you practice mantra, please don't quarrel with yourself. If your mind is running into fantasies, let it go. You expect the mind to be calm like a moonlit night, free from clouds and thunder. That's not possible. When you practice your mantra, please remember that you are not practicing it to stop this eternal process, to crush the basis of your faculties, your knowledge, and your enlightenment. To crush the mind is to kill life. To suppress an emotion is to destroy the very base of your ambition and desire. Man cannot be anything unless he has the whole mind to work from. The greatest discoveries in history, the greatest victories, the greatest paintings, compositions, and realisations, they are all products of the mind. The mind is constantly resonating, vibrating with all kinds of impressions, even now, but you don't see it, you don't know it, because your senses are engaged. As soon as you isolate your mind, you can see the whole beautiful game it constantly plays. The more you evolve in spiritual life, the more you become aware of the homogeneity of the mind. So therefore, in Mantra, do not aim at killing any of the expressions of the mind. Mind is not your problem at all – you are the mind's problem, always wanting more experiences. So whenever you practice mantra, yantra or kriya yoga, please remember that you are not going to fight with the mind.

CHAPTER 7

Beneficial Effects of 'Om Namah Mantra' Mantra

7.1 Beneficial Effects of Chanting Om Namah Shivaya: An Introduction

Excluding 'OM' Om Namah Shivaya is a five-syllable mantra (Panchakshari Mantra), dedicated to Lord Shiva. The effect of chanting Om Namah Shivaya is that it connects you with the true blissfulness. It is considered to be one of the most important sounds in all the universe and has been chanted for thousands of years. It is believed that this leads to profound enlightenment. But there are more than just these benefits of this powerful, ancient practice.

Om is the first sound that emerged from the vibrations of the cosmic energy that created the Universe. It is the representation of the Creator. Om Namah Shivaya is self-begotten, that is, it is on its own and doesn't need another syllable to make its sound. Chanting Om Namah Shivaya will give you a sense of the source of the Universe, and when chanted right, Om's sound reverberates through your body, filling it with energy and tranquillity. Details of this magical word 'OM' have already been discussed in an earlier chapter.

Whilst most people in today's world are plagued by stress and tension - it has become a necessity for people to find their recluse, a place of peace and perhaps, sweating it out from your soul, detoxifying yourself from within. Om Namah Shivaya is not merely a chant — it's a cult; self-existing. It's purification of the soul through sound. Om Namah Shivaya is the sound of sounds — an opening to the multiverse. You can call it a medicinal chant; you can name it the soul singer. Name it whatever, but the sweet sound of Om Namah Shivaya is untouched by any adjectives addressed.

When you sing or chant Om Namah Shivaya, it makes your heart sing along, it makes your soul reverberate in its own reality. Beginning from the root OM, the sound of the Universe itself — Om Namah Shivaya is peace and sanctity in its own waking reality. The sound of both; the Universe and the Multiverse and we are multi-dimensional beings expanding our wings through it.

Whenever you are distressed in life or feel restless or when you lose track of yourself and have nowhere to go - the time when all you want is peace but it chooses to abandon you, merely drown in the sweet sound of Om Namah Shivaya and you shall be saved.

When something so positive and ethereal surrounds you even the negativity in its complex form is merely left charred to its residual form. The chant of Om Namah Shivaya heals you and sends you in a transcendental mode.

When you feel that life is conspiring against you and there is no peace left, this mantra will show you the path to peace and give you the clarity and intellect needed to respond with grace and dignity.

Om Namah Shivaya mantra tempers your ego and aggression; it shows you the right path and relieves stress from your overburdened mind. According to astrology, this Mantra is very powerful in diminishing the harmful effects of the negative "grahas" (planets) and thus, it minimizes any bad influence on your natal chart that you might beget from the negative influence of these planets.

It is most beneficial to chant this mantra in the morning and the evening, however, it not just restricted to these hours one can chant the mantra anytime, anywhere especially when faced with negative forces or in trouble. In the previous chapter the timings of chanting this mantra are discussed in details.

7.2 Some Beneficial Effects of Chanting 'Om Namah Shivaya' Mantra

- Chanting Om Namah Shivaya stabilizes your thoughts.
- Om Namah Shivaya makes you feel light and reduce the heaviness of life.
- Om Namah Shivaya improves your voice by giving strength to your vocal cords and the muscles around it. It produces a vibration and sound which is felt through your vocal cords and sinuses. The vibrations open up the sinuses to clear the airways.
- Your spinal cord is strengthened through the vibrations caused by Om Namah Shivaya. As this sound is

generated from the abdomen, it helps to strengthen the supporting muscles of the spinal cord.

- Om Namah Shivaya chanting benefits the thyroid glands and the throat.
- It helps in controlling your senses and anxieties.
- Om Namah Shivaya has cardiovascular benefits – by relaxing your mind and body; your blood pressure will decrease and your heart will beat with a regular rhythm.
- It gives calmness to your mind.
- Om Namah Shivaya purifies the environment around you and creates positive vibrations.
- It gives you better immunity and self-healing power.
- Chanting Om Namah Shivaya improves your concentration and helps you focus.
- Chanting Om Namah Shivaya gives you deep relaxation.
- It is said that rubbing your hands together while chanting Om Namah Shivaya and putting those charged hands on different parts of the body heals or activates those body parts.
- Chanting Om Namah Shivaya gives you better control over your emotions, thus allowing you to see situations with a clear and rational mind.
- When chanting Om Namah Shivaya in a group, the effects are amplified and this will produce immense positive vibrations which charge up the entire vicinity.

- This mantra is also known as the beeja mantra and helps you to bring desired results and wishes.
- This mantra helps to cure depression.
- When you chant this mantra, its vibration helps you to prevent stroke and serious brain injury.
- Om Namah Shivaya reduces the chances of heart strokes and organ failure.
- Om Namah Shivaya can even help cleanse your skin. The massive levels of internal positive energy and a cleansed aura that come from chanting Om Namah Shivaya regularly will be reflected externally with a sunny glow on your face and body.
- If you're looking at the spiritual eye while chanting, the effects of chanting Om Namah Shivaya will awaken your third eye.
- Chanting Om Namah Shivaya increases the happiness chemical which is known as GABA chemical.
- Chanting Om Namah Shivaya gives you eternal joy.
- Chanting Om Namah Shivaya mantra makes you free from your animal passion and rude behaviour.
- Chanting Om Namah Shivaya heals your sorrows, emotional pain and takes you out of grief.
- Om Namah Shivaya spreads positivity in your house. Worshipping Shiva in the home brings happiness into the family.

- Chanting Om Namah Shivaya is believed to free you from your past sins.
- It detoxifies your body by getting rid of the toxins, keeping you young and fresh.
- Shiva Namah Mantra is a very powerful mantra that gives benefits even by listening. Its music is so calm that you will forget everything for sometimes.
- This Mantra has a deep effect on the mind, sometimes you sing it unknowingly.
- It quickly cleans your mind, throws out negative thoughts and makes you fresh.
- This Mantra improves every aspect of life, from material things to health to the soul's happiness.
- True satisfaction can be achieved because the chanting of this mantra makes ourselves devotional which is most important for the soul.
- In the universe, nothing which can't be achieved for true devotee because Lord Shiva is beyond our universe and creates everything from nothing.
- Protection is provided by chanting of this Mantra by Mahadeva, an eternal God.
- Chanting it will fill life with divinity and peace.
- Listening and chanting this mantra, will connect us to God Shiva because every time when we chant it, we praise God, respect them, think about them.

- Trouble is reduced. Due to previous Karma, one faces sorrow in life but by chanting this mantra and remembering Lord Shiva, problems are reduced, the effect of bad karma is reduced.

- This Mantra has such powers which deeply impacts the inner system of the body, its vibration and energy improve brain, speaking ability, thinking, breathing.

- The Mantra is Moksha Giver and stabilizes your thoughts – The Chanting of Om Namah Shivaya is not just moksha giving mantra, it also enlightens, our inner thoughts process and improves blood circulation on the neurons. In medical terms, this concept is called neuroplasticity.

- When someone chants Om Namah Shivaya, at that moment he becomes AGHORI. Ghor means extreme and, AGhor (Not Ghor) means the one who is not extreme. That's how Shiva makes you feel light inside your heart.

- A significant vibration originates in the subconsciousness part of the mind which gives the feeling of internal ecstasy. Om Namah Shivaya mantra benefits that the continuous repetition of the divine mantra is the way toward perennial joy.

- Om Namah Shivaya helps in controlling senses and anxieties. Neelakantham is Vairagya founder (Means founder of dispassion). Shiva Kaam Bhasmam (Destroyer of eroticism) makes you qualify to control your senses and nerves. The deity of eroticism (Kaam Dev) will not influence you.

- Lord Shiva holds moon crescent on his head. It impacts chanter body when somebody starts Om Namah Shivaya chanting. It cools his/her mind and helps one to get peace of mind, persistence, and calmness especially when everything is going against you.
- People who lack happiness chemicals always feel exhausted. The frontal area of the human brain is in the Orbito prefrontal cortex which is responsible for making decisions, problem-solving and awakening the consciousness gets charged by chanting of Om Namah Shivaya mantra.
- Students get the immense benefit in improving memory-power after the Om Namah Shivaya chanting. Therefore if your kids are suffering from low memory power, advise them to chant the mantra for 15 mins every day.
- Chanting Om Namah Shivaya mantra gives you eternal joy.
- Shiva becomes your protector, Every kind of panic, stress, depression, insanity starts fading slowly, when you begin Om Namah Shivaya chanting. Lord Himself becomes the protector of the chanter.
- Om Namah Shivaya mantra grows positive energy in you which improves your body metabolism and reduces the toxicity of the body. You will start feeling the reduction in your aggression and anger. You require to practice mantra with high reverence on Shiva.

- Slowly–Slowly, internal and external changes start appearing. This mantra activates the inactive neurons of the brain cell. Your body and skin start getting glow and shine by tightening up your pores automatically in a natural way. Om Namah Shivaya is a powerful maha-mantra.

- The continuous 108-times repetition is more beneficial to get Siddhis (Urja or strength). It is helpful in awakening Kundalini Yoga Shakti.

- Health Benefits of Om Namah Shivaya chanting improves your blood circulation and stabilizes heartbeat.

- Mantra can even enhance your blood purification system. Chanting the mantra also purifies your rationalizing process which improves your physiological as well as intellectual well-being.

- It also heals your sorrows, emotional pain and takes you out of the darkness and show the positivity of life.

- It also reduces the chances of heart strokes and organ failure.

- It spreads positivity in your house Worshipping Shiva in the home brings happiness into the family. Shiva & Shakti both get established in that house. You start understanding others' problems and you become ever ready to give helping hand to others. Moral values will start growing in the kids. Positive vibes will get radiating from that home and from the people living in that home. Chanting Om Namah Shivaya makes the law of attraction works better in your favour.

- The Power of Om Namah Shivaya is such that it can free you from your past sins.
- The Mantra helps you to invoke Atmya-Gyan. What most of the people don't know is that almighty Shiva is known for his simplicity and guiltless nature. This mantra helps you to get connected with supreme consciousness. Every substance including deities is the manifestation of Shiva's energy. Chanting Om Namah Shivaya is like worshipping the primary elements.
- It is for God Shiva who is great, who knows everything, who is omnipresent and who protects the whole world.
- It is for giving respect and invocation to Lord Shiva.
- Om Namah Shivaya mantra gives incredible power and effect if you chanted 108 times.
- It gives exponential benefits of chanted 1008 times.
- It is a way to get unimaginable knowledge and power.
- The power and effect of this mantra are infinite that is impossible to even describe.
- God is with him everywhere who worshipping and chanting Om Namah Shivaya every time.
- Meditation with chanting 'Om Namah Shivaya' increases concentration and memory; neurons in the brain affected by chanting a mantra.

- It is scientifically proven the benefits of meditation and chanting on concentration ability and focusing ability.
- Om Namah Shivaya infuses positive energy and removes negative energy. It is also a stress-buster, helping you to relax and unwind.
- A restless mind becomes stable and peaceful with regular chanting.
- Om Namah Shivaya helps you to gain control over your senses. This will help you govern your mind eventually.
- Om Namah Shivaya gives you a sense of direction and purpose in life.
- There are nine planets and 27 constellations. Since the Shiva Tattva is the presiding energy and governs the planets as well, chanting Om Namah Shivaya can help nullify the effects of malefic planets to a certain extent.
- Om Namah Shivaya gives you a sense of direction and purpose in life.
- This mantra is associated with qualities of prayer, divine-love, grace, truth, and blissfulness. When done correctly, it calms the mind and brings spiritual insight and knowledge. It also keeps the devotee close to Shiva and within His protective global fellowship.
- Traditionally, it is accepted to be a powerful healing mantra beneficial for all physical and mental ailments. Soulful recitation of this mantra brings peace to the heart and joy to the Ātman or soul. Many Hindu

> teachers consider that the recitation of these syllables is sound therapy for the body and nectar for the Ātman. The nature of the mantra is the calling upon the higher Self; it is the calling upon Shiva.

Students have tension in their studies.; and tension to get good marks and a high score in the examinations. But not all students can be successful. Not all people achieve success in a job. It creates anxiety and grief. It reduces our performance. But Chanting Om Namah Shivaya 1008 time or only 108 times removes the grief and anxiety from the life.

This means that you could lose focus while studying, or lose focus while working at your job, or you could easily be distracted from achieving your goals. Having optimal focus in life is extremely important. Fortunately, the "Om Namah Shivaya" mantra can help you to become completely focused on your task at hand as it activates all your chakras and allows you to think much better. We get a steady mind and supernatural intelligence to achieve peace. It also helps you to concentrate on a particular thing at a time very clearly. This means you will end up with better grades, more tremendous success at your job, and an improved direction towards achieving your goals.

7.3 Improved Gratitude

We might not realize it, but we often become very ungrateful in our lives. It is essential for every individual to realize how blessed they are. Our lords have blessed us in so many ways. If you are a healthy individual who can breathe, eat, sleep, walk and sit properly, then you are very blessed.

If you have a roof above your head, food to eat, clean water to drink, and a source of education or income, then you are among the luckiest people in the world. However, we often take these things for granted and don't show our gratitude to God. But chanting the "Om Namah Shivaya" mantra will promote a sense of thankfulness and appreciation within you.

You can have a perfect and happy life if you are thankful for everything you have because then even the lord will be pleased with you and he will give you more. These positive energies and vibes can be generated with the help of the "Om Namah Shivaya" mantra.

7.4 Increased Faith in God

Shiva is the great lord of the Universe. The existence of Shiva is similar to that of nothingness. It is the matter that makes up space, planets, and stars, and this is the matter that is the most common throughout the universe. Therefore, Lord Shiva is present everywhere, and with the help of this great God, we can achieve a lot in our lives.

Chanting the **"Om Namah Shivaya"** mantra is our way of remembering the great lord Shiva and showing our faith, trust and thankfulness to him. Furthermore, if you chant this mantra regularly, you will be bestowed with greater success and happiness in life. Lord Shiva will give you the strength, power, and knowledge to achieve all your goals, along with bestowing their blessings upon you to have a peaceful and happy life.

Om Namah Shivaya vibration benefits us to get supernatural intelligence to achieve peace.

The effects of chanting om Namah Shivaya have also been confirmed by scientists and they verified that daily frequently chanting OM Namah Shivaya mantra decreases stress, enhances concentration, gives peace of mind, and manages depression. It was concluded in the summary that this mantra works as a brain stabilizer which is energy medicine for those under stress.

Chanting this mantra is quite simple and the benefits of it are quite magical. Only condition what a person needs is a complete faith and belief. There are certain ways, however, you can make this worth your while – Ideally, you should chant this mantra 108 times. You should sit with your legs folded – that is the Yoga pose, with your back straight. As you wake up early in the morning and cleanse yourself with your daily bathing ritual, sit in open air and breathe in nature. It is ideal to sit with the chanting beads and chant the mantra 108 times.

The mantra Om Namah Shivaya is the way to tap into your infinite space and boundless potential locked inside of you. This mantra not only brings peace but your personal sanctuary. Shiva is the Universe and Multiverse – a waking reality and as you chant this mantra, you also send love vibrations to the Cosmos itself and it is bound to come back to you ten folds.

Om Namah Shivaya means 'I bow down to Shiva', implying that one is bowing down to his own consciousness because Shiva in his essence is the consciousness that resides in us all. Shiva represents the inner self and that is why He is also the destroyer or the ultimate. Shiva is the womb from which everything comes out and eventually goes back to it. In this mantra, the devout bows down to Shiva, his own true self that is. Om Namah Shivaya is the sound of the inner being, thus.

It is believed that Om Namah Shivaya is the ultimate mantra, the most powerful and most magical. If it continually reverberates in your heart, there is absolutely no need to perform austerities or to even perform Yoga. Also, the most beautiful aspect of this mantra is that you do not need to perform any rituals or need a particular time. This mantra is akin to meditating and when combined with meditation followed by the sound of Om Namah Shivaya, it is the eternal bliss we keep searching for our entire life. As this mantra becomes the part and parcel of your life you will notice many positive changes in your life.

Well, have you ever given it a thought what it is to feel not bound by time? To not feel caged and feel like you have lost it all? There is a sweet secret to chanting God's name. When you chant Shiva's name over and over, you vibrate in his consciousness and you become Him and He becomes you. Yes, you beautifully merge with the Cosmos itself. Not just this but merely chanting Om Namah Shivaya reduces almost 99.9 percent of negative effects that one begets due to astral positions of the planets. In ancient times, Om Namah Shivaya was considered to be a healing mantra for all mental or physical ailments. Soulful chanting of this mantra brings joy and peace to your heart and much peace and sanctity to your soul, awakening the Atman that you are. Sages believe that the sound of this mantra is sound therapy to the body and potent nectar for the Atman.

When you chant Om Namah Shivaya, it is basically calling upon your higher Self – when you call upon Shiva, the destroyer of the deity, aid in death – the harbinger of peace in the multiverse, you are most connected with yourself and your higher being and there is no lie in the fire that you ignite whilst chanṭing this soulful mantra that is akin to life itself –

OM NAMAH SHIAVAYA:

I bow down to Shiva;
The World bows down to Shiva;
The Universe Bows down to Shiva.

Bibliography

Dudeja, Jai Paul. "An Overview of Primordial, Apaurusheya, Perennial, Universal 'OM' Mantra and Its Scientific Analysis", International Journal of Current Trends in

Dudeja, Jai Paul. "Chakras Healing and Kundalini Awakening by Yogic Techniques", Chaukhamba Sanskrit Pratishthan, Delhi, 2022.

Dudeja, Jai Paul. "Gayatri Mantra: A GPS to Enlightenment", Adhyayan Publishers and Distributors, New Delhi, 2018.

Dudeja, Jai Paul. "Maha Mrityunjaya Mantra: An Invincible Armour for Conquering Death", Kalpaz Publications, New Delhi, 2018.

Dudeja, Jai Paul. "Meditation Practices across the Globe and Their Beneficial Effects", White Falcon Publishing, 2021.

Dudeja, Jai Paul. "Scientific Analysis of Mantra-Based Meditation and Its Beneficial Effects: An Overview", International Journal of Advanced Scientific Technologies in Engineering and Management Sciences (IJASTEMS-ISSN: 2454-356X), Vol. 3, Issue 6, June 2017, pp. 21-26. WorldCat Unique Identifier # 7374726082.

Dudeja, Jai Paul. "Significance of the Auspicious Number 1008", International Journal of Yogic, Human Movement and Sports Sciences, (ISSN: 2456-4419, Impact Factor 5.18),Vol. 3, Issue. 1, 2018, pp 825-829.

Dudeja, Jai Paul. "Spiritual and Scientific Significance of the Number 108", International Journal of Yogic, Human Movement and Sports Sciences, (ISSN: 2456-4419),Vol. 3, Issue. 1, 2018, pp 611-615.

Dudeja, Jai Paul. "The Third Eye: A Spiritual Laser for Stimulating Inner Awakening", GenNext Publication, New Delhi, 2019.

Pereira, Contzen. "A comparative study of frequencies of a Buddhist mantra– Om Mani Padme Hum and a Hindu mantra – Om Namah Shivaya", IJISET - International Journal of Innovative Science, Engineering & Technology, Vol. 3 Issue 4, April 2016.

Roy, Priya P. Roy, Kumar Sai Sailesh, Archana R, Soumya Mishra, Arati Amin, Sabu Thomas, Udaya Kumar Reddy and Supriya Rajan. " Om Namah Shivaya for Management of Stress in Elderly Women with Hypertension", International J. Pharmaceutical Sciences and Research, Volume 12, December 2021.

Sadhguru, "Shiva – Ultimate Outlaw", ©2014 Sadhguru, First Edition: February 2014 Science and Technology, (ISSN: 0976-9730),Vol. 7, Issue. 9, Sep 2017, pp 20370-20390.

Sivananda, Swami and Swami Satyananda "Mantra", Rikhiapeeth, 2015.

Sri Swami Sivananda. "Lord Siva and His Worship", A Divine Life Publication, 1996.

Index

www.ingramcontent.com/pod-product-compliance
Ingram Content Group UK Ltd.
Pitfield, Milton Keynes, MK11 3LW, UK
UKHW012248290726
14090UKWH00013B/528